Libro de Colorear para Adultos

MANDALA
Perros y Gatos

50 Imàgenes de Colorear para Aliviar el Estrés

Copyright © 2022 – Wonderful Press
All rights reserved

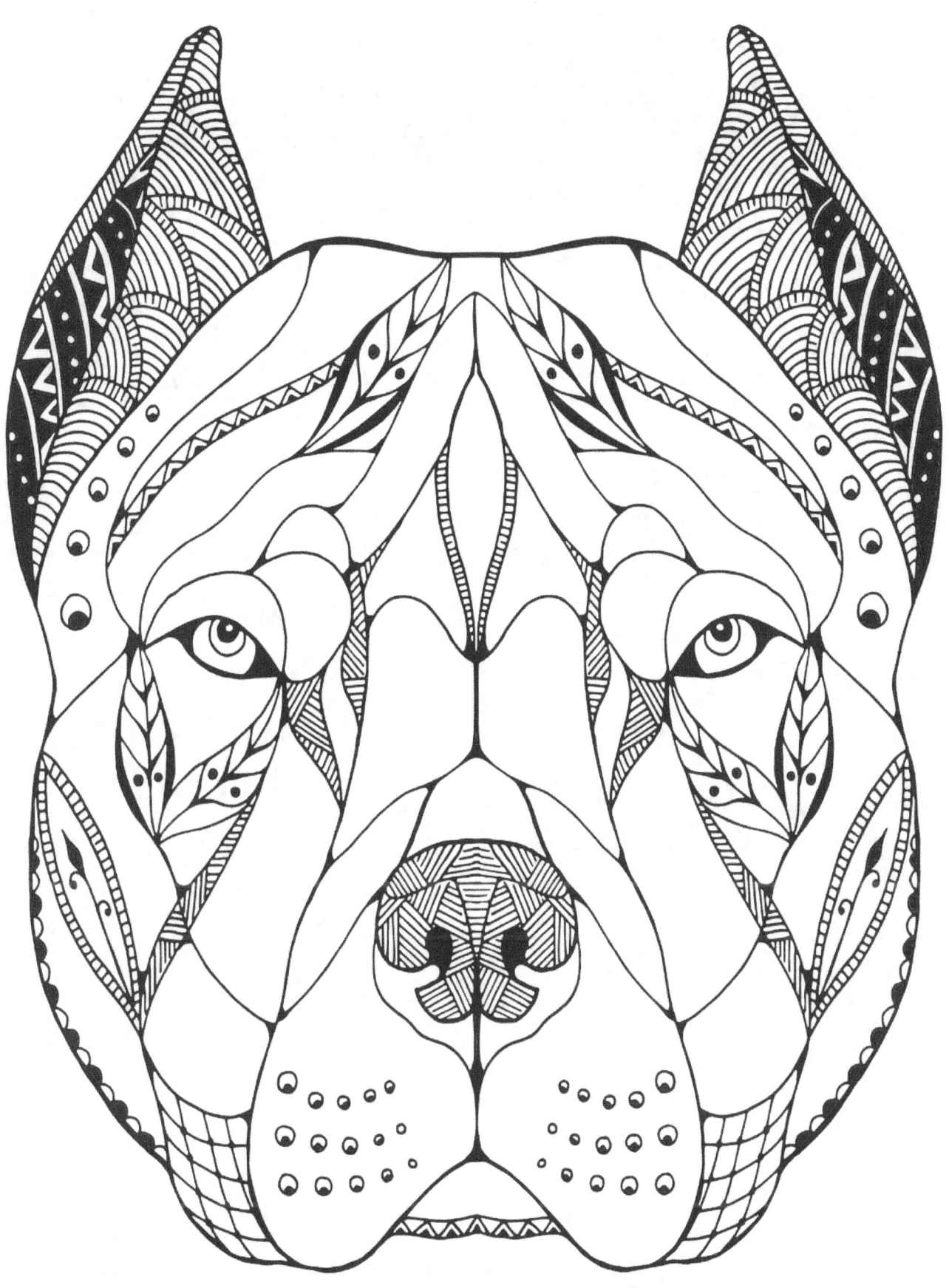

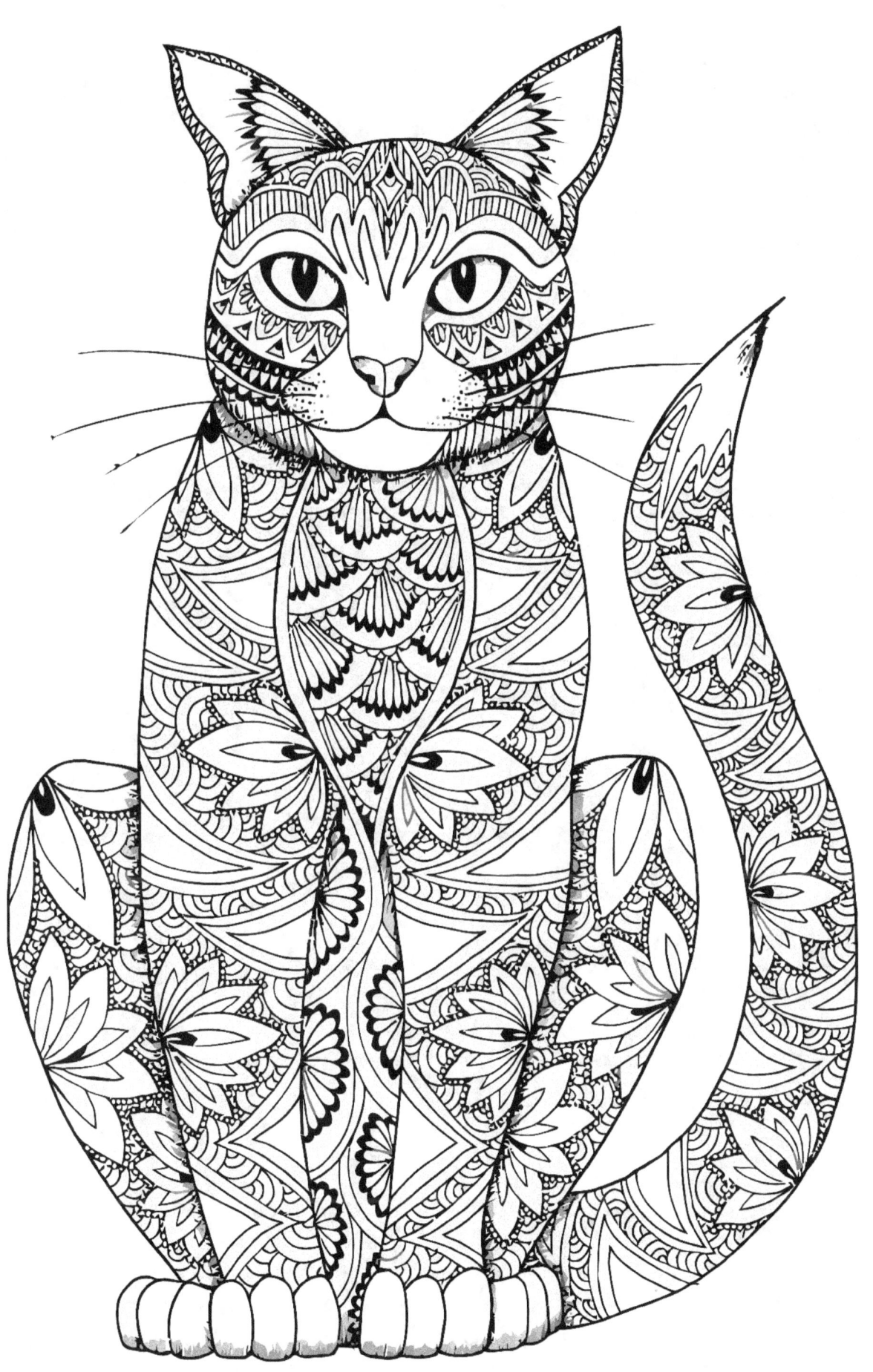

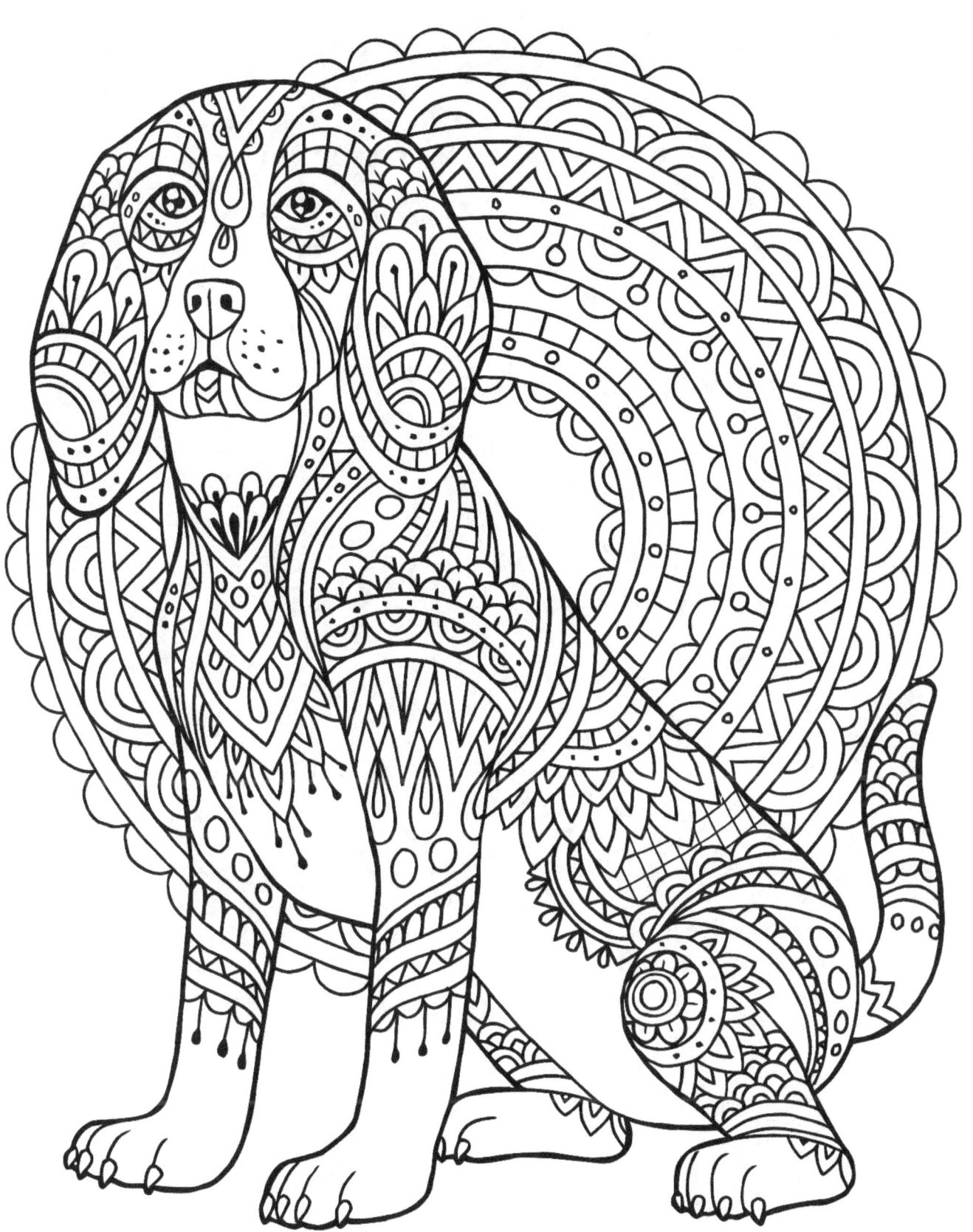

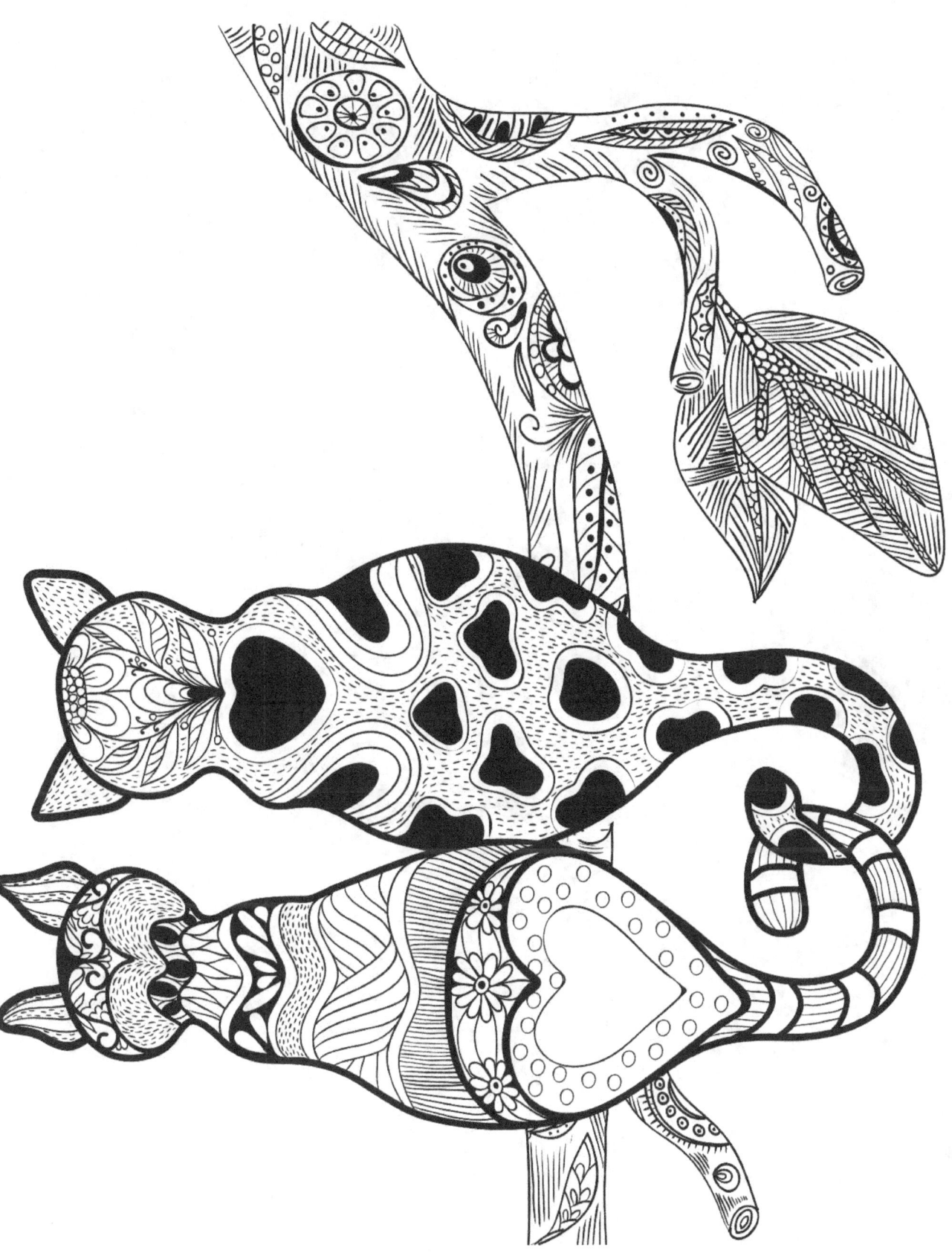

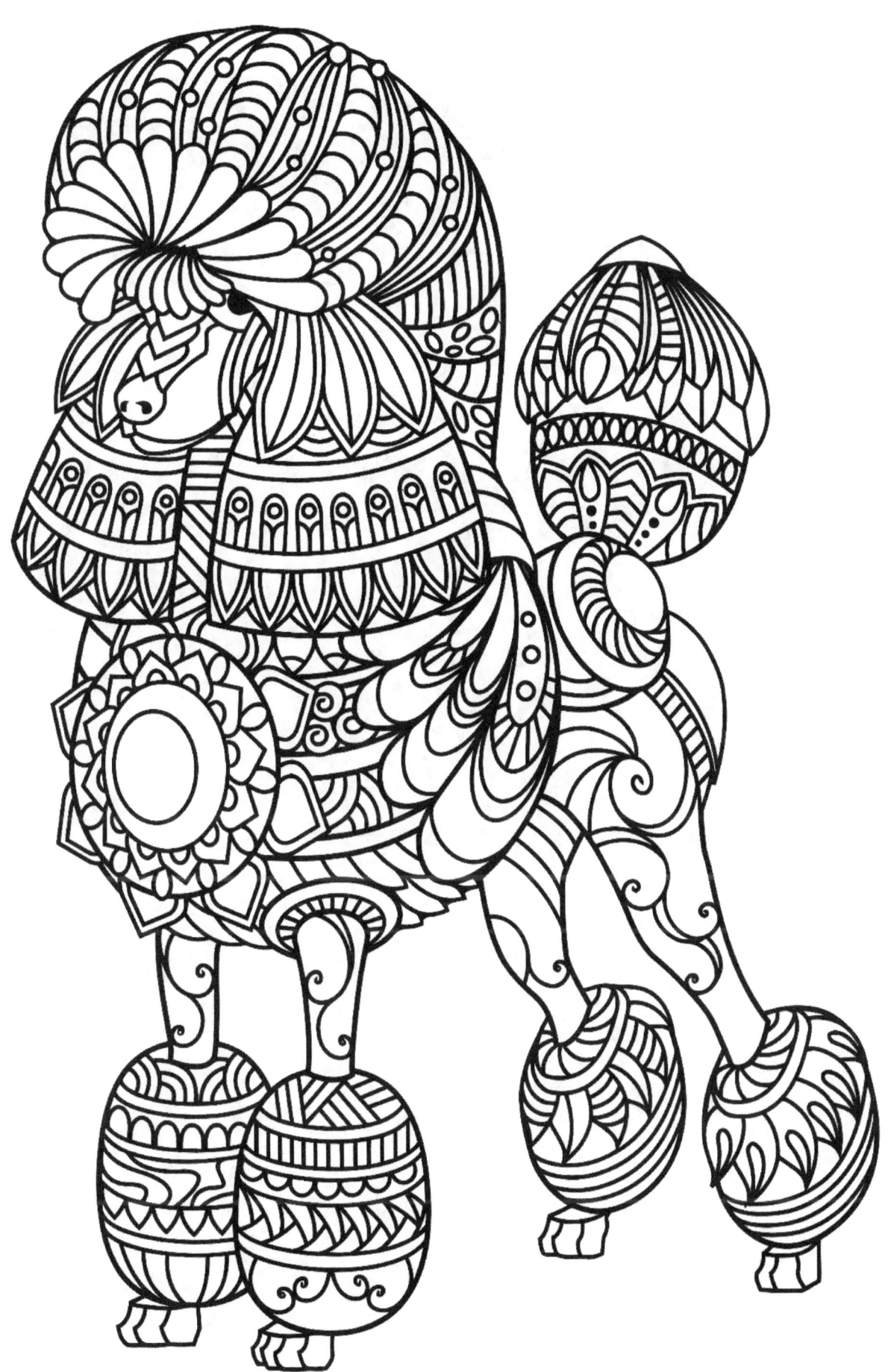

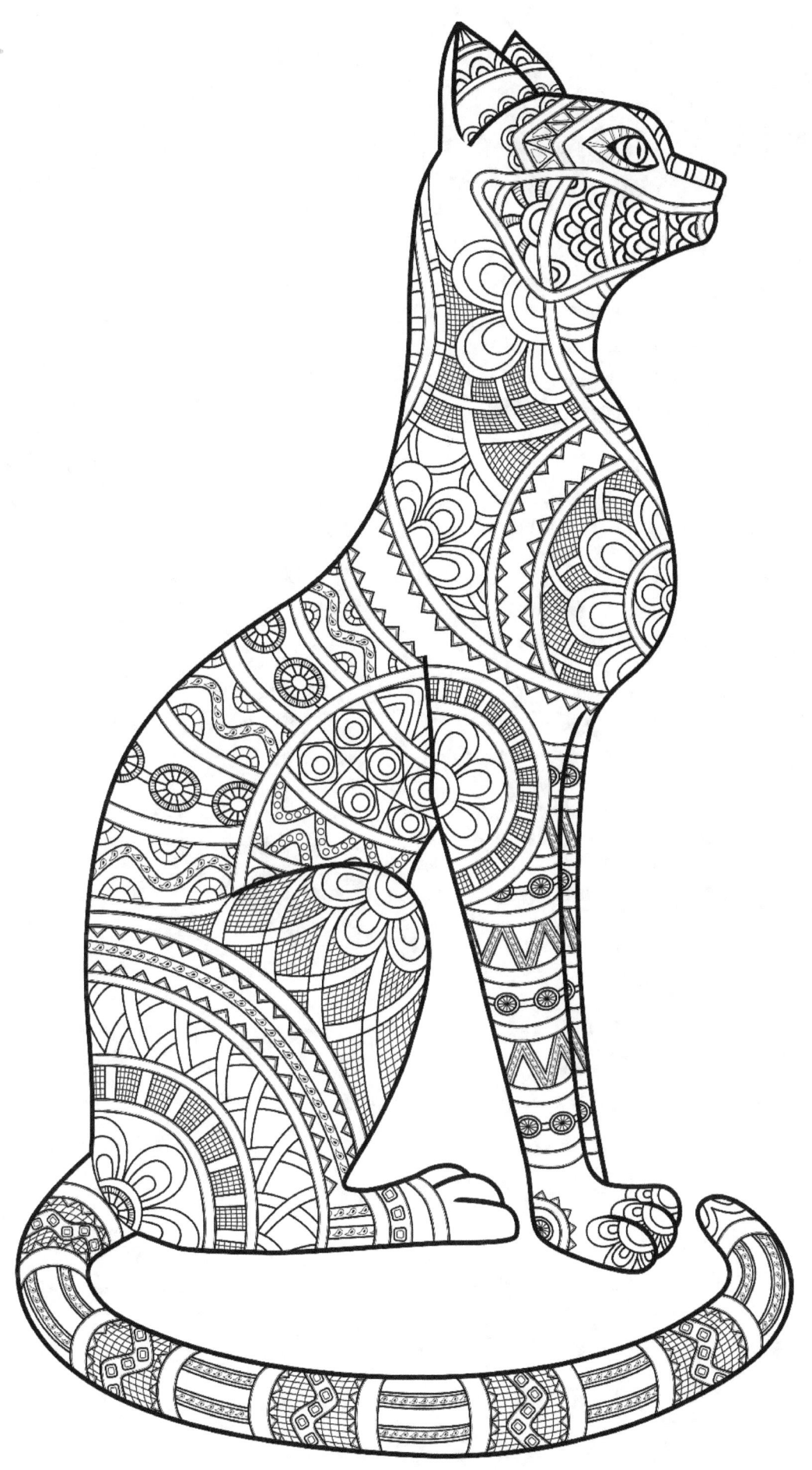

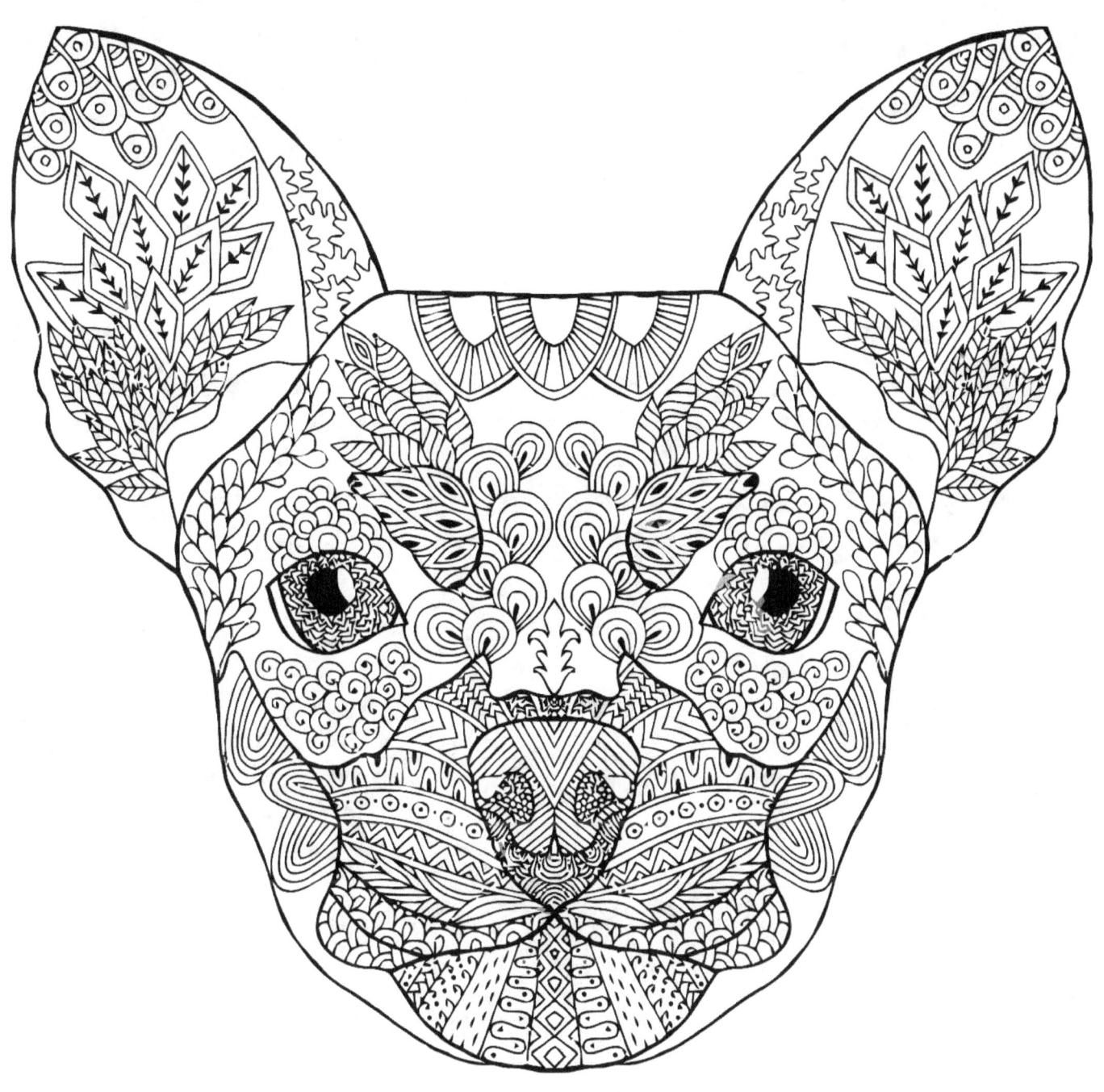

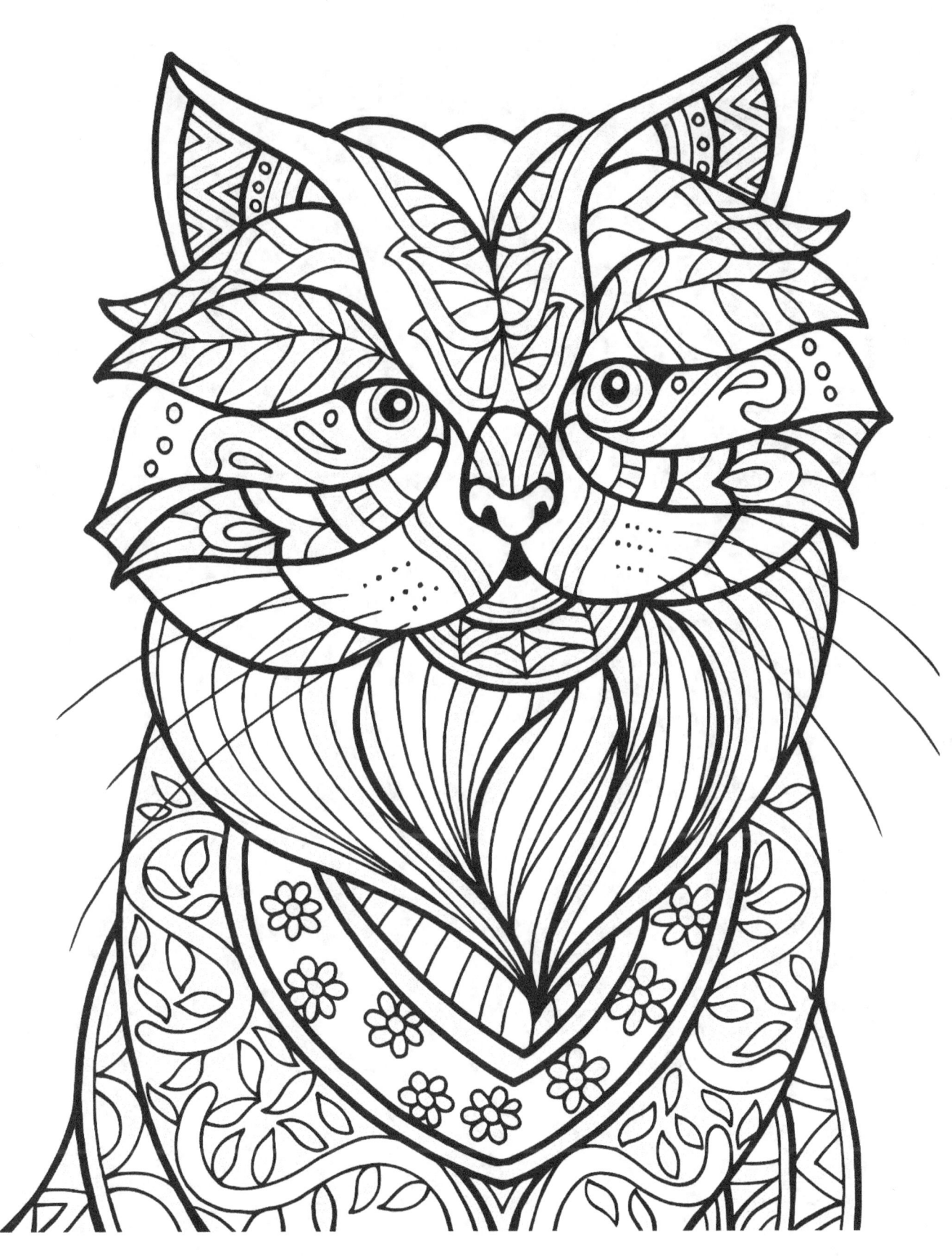

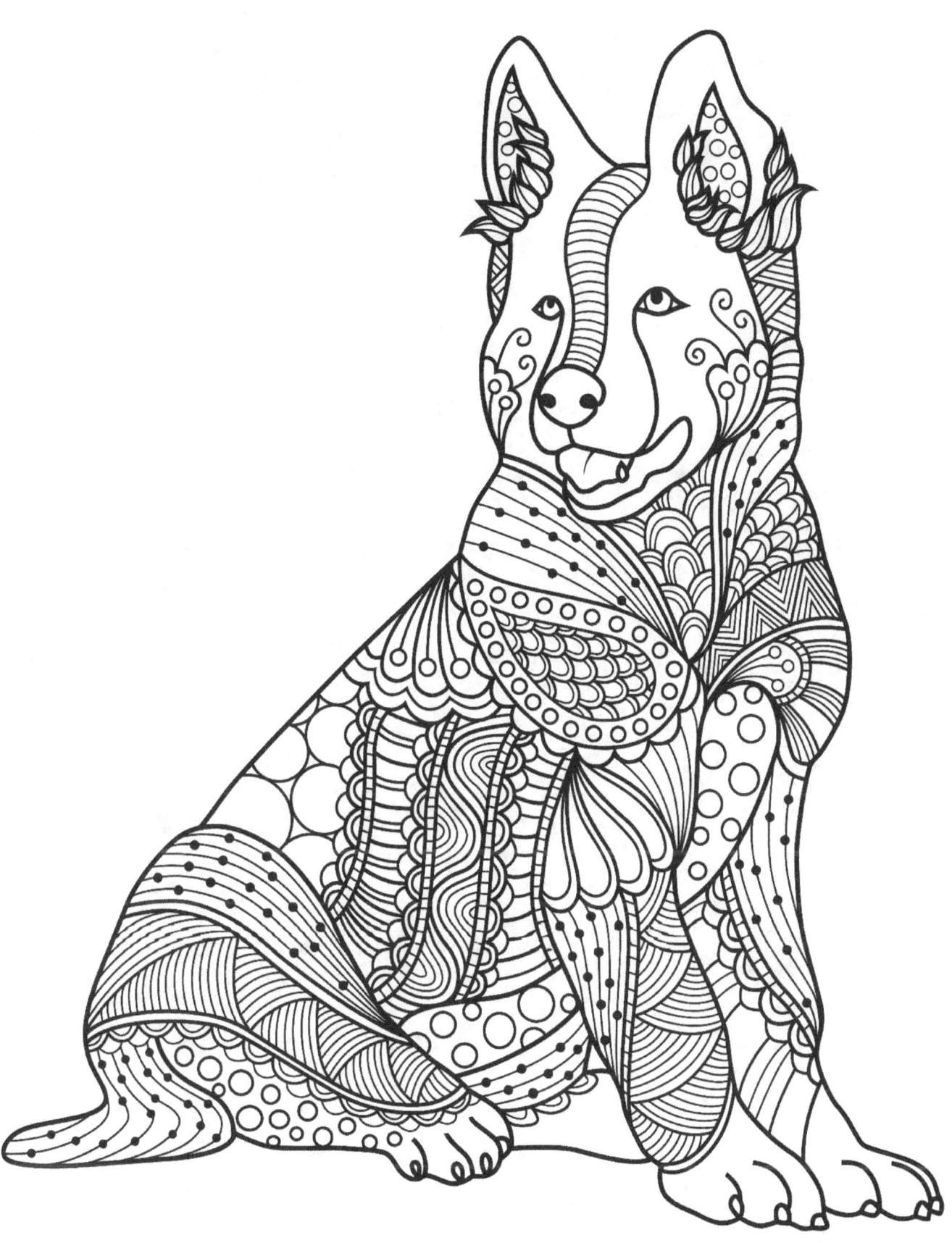

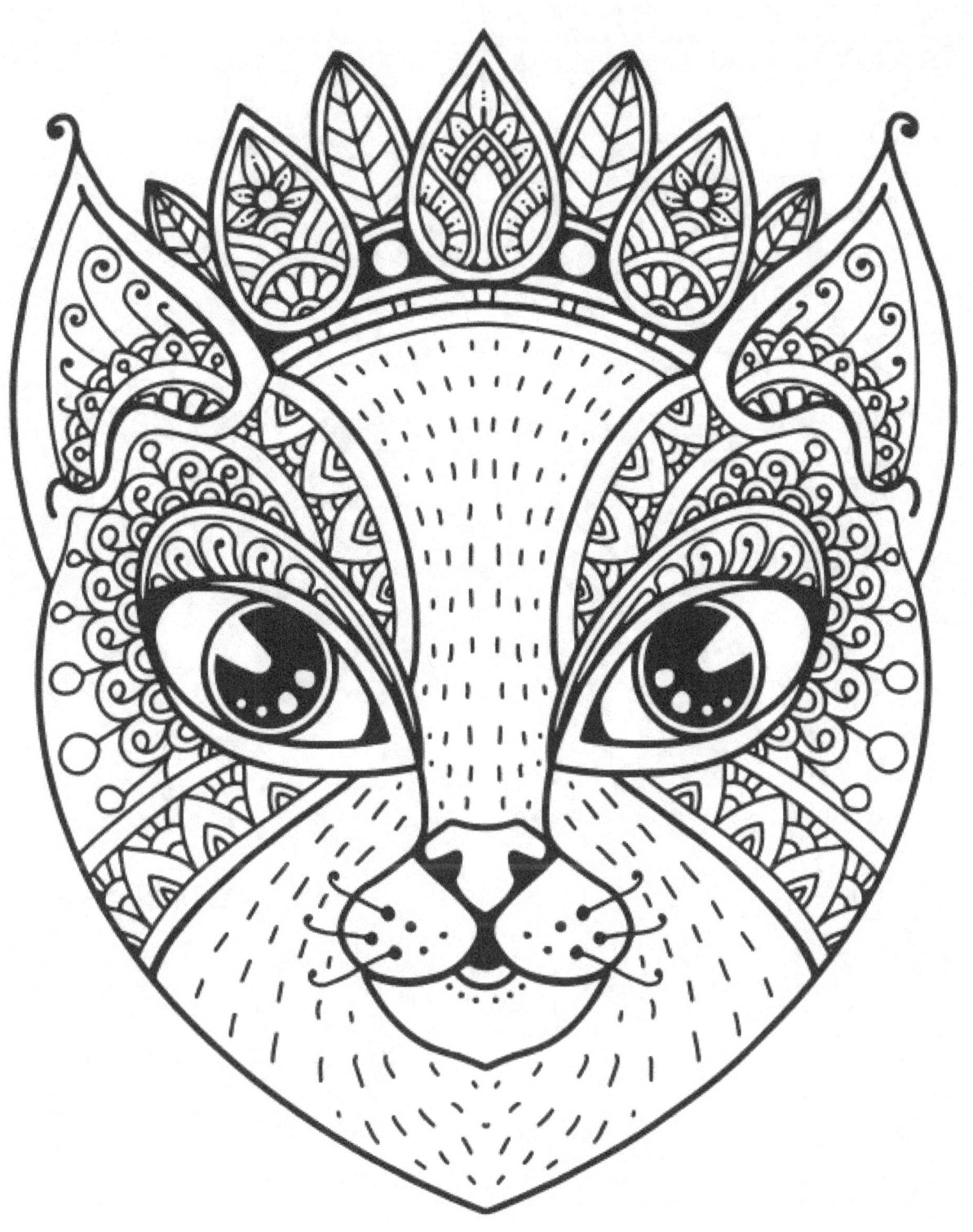

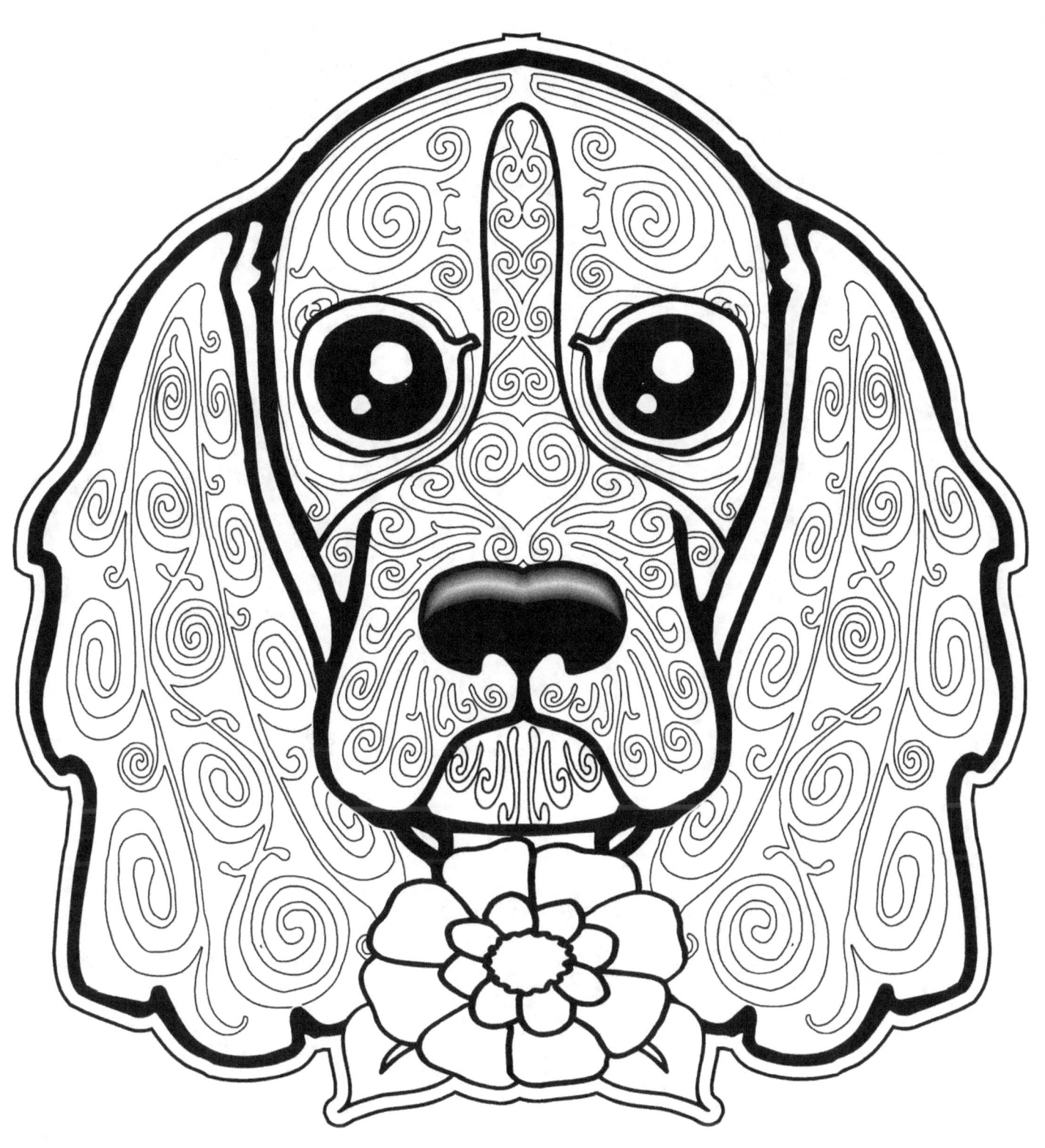

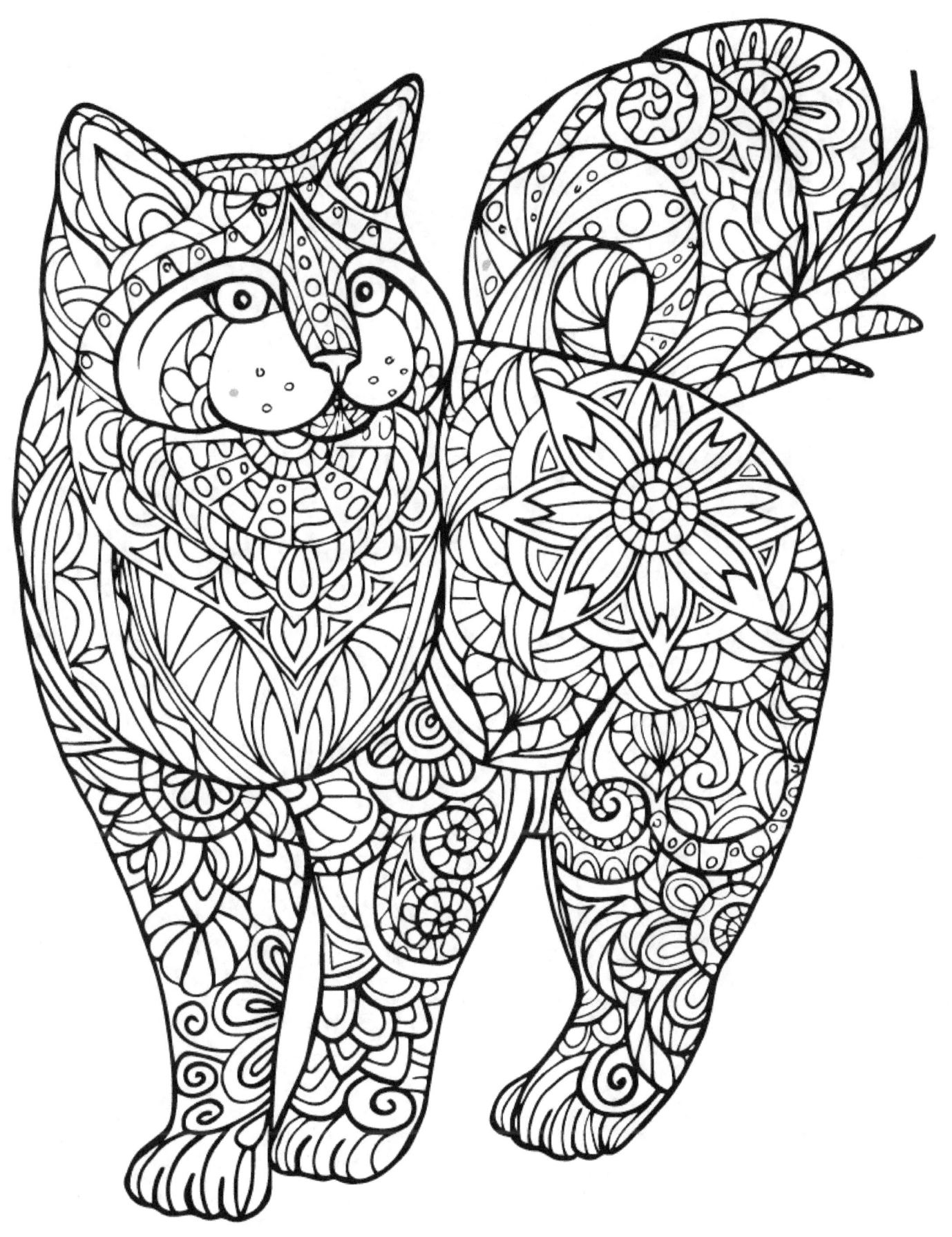

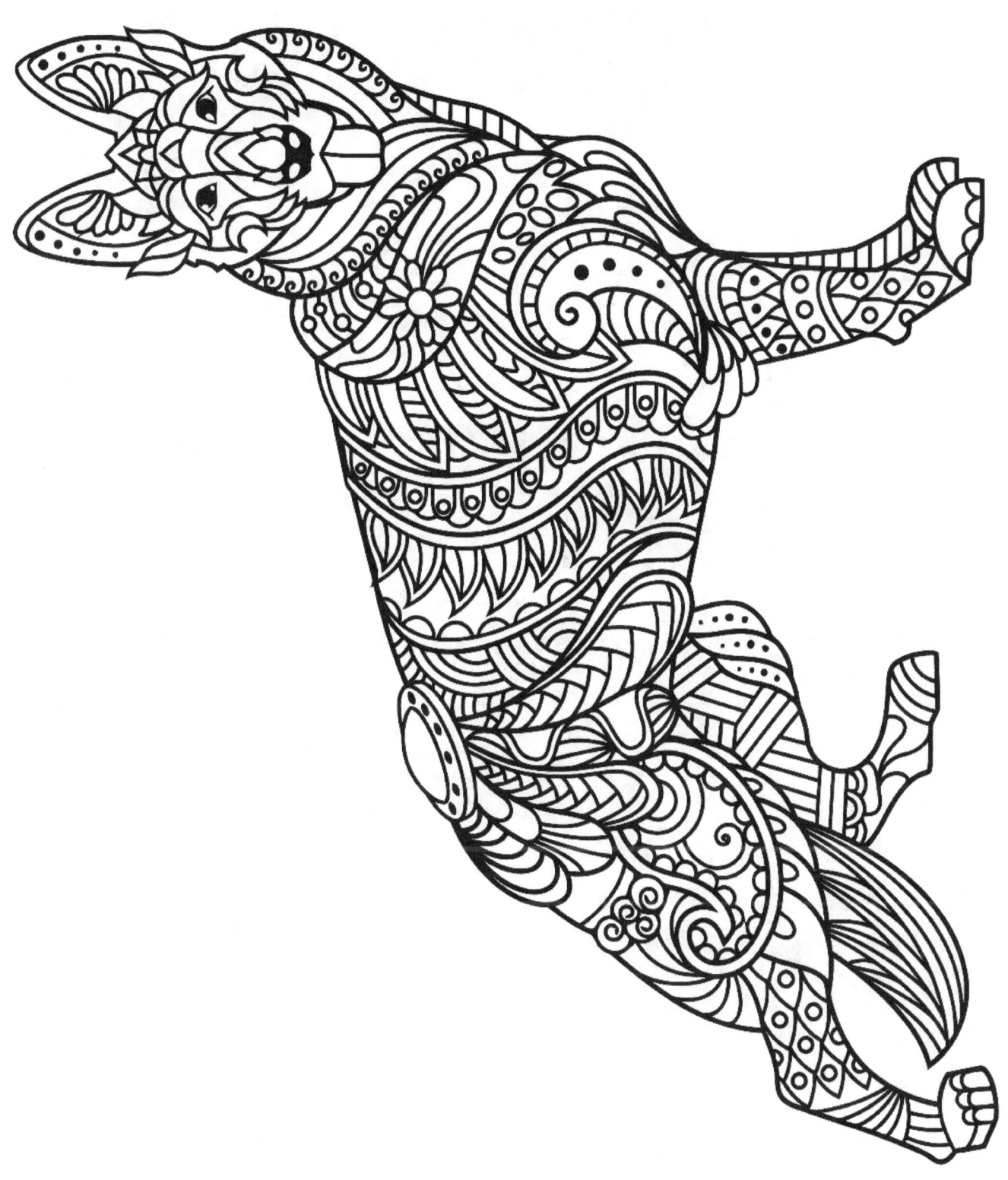

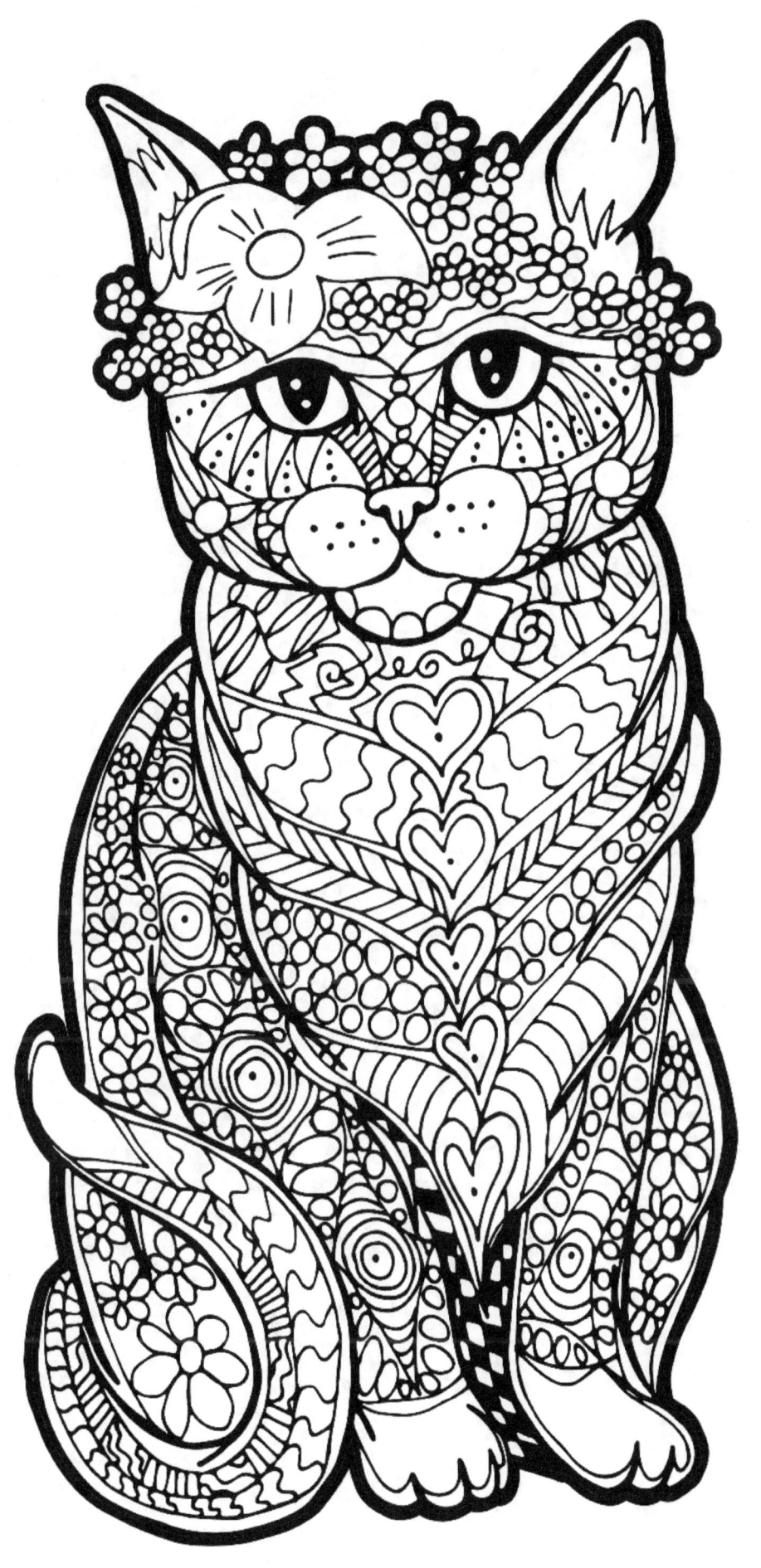

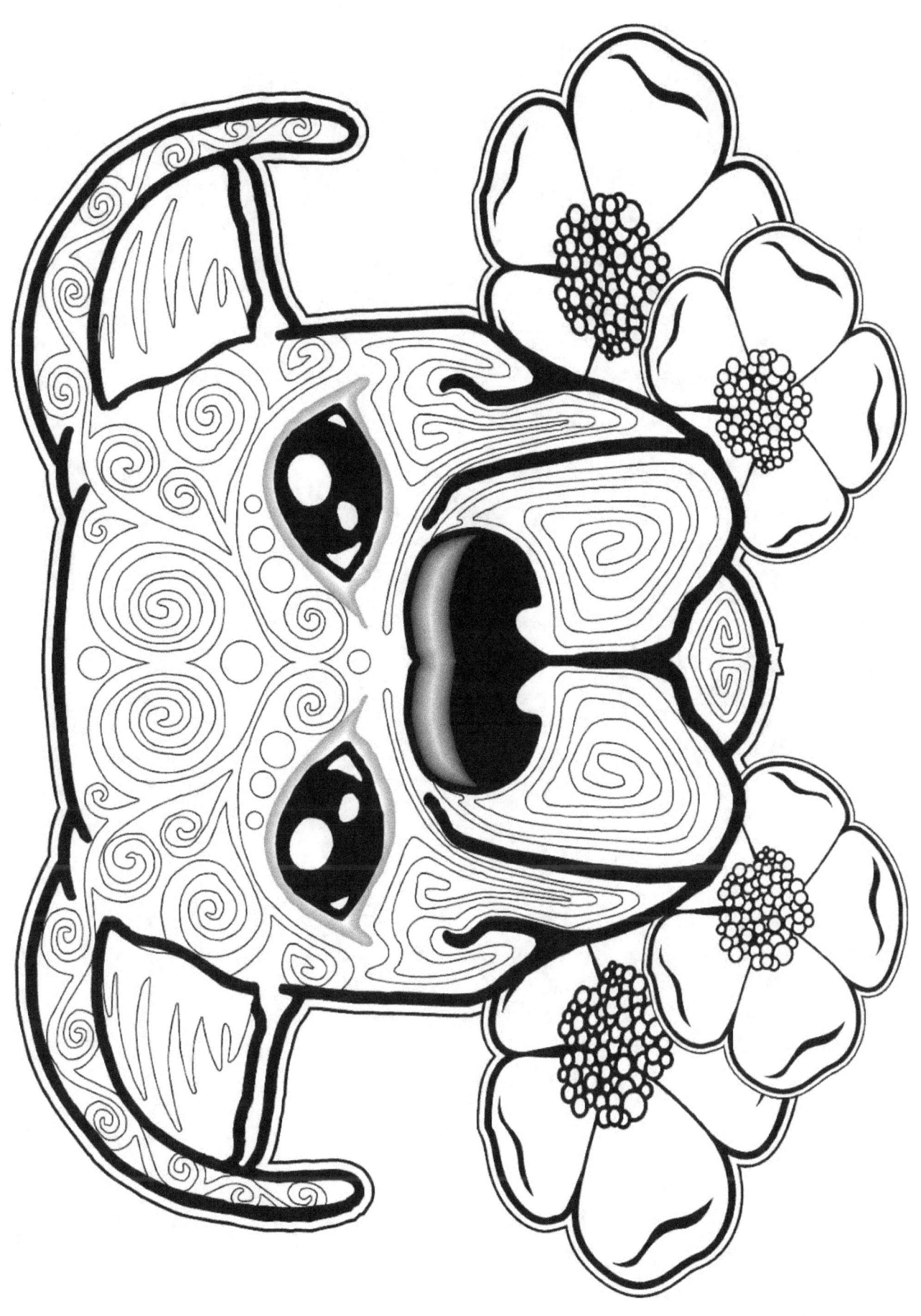

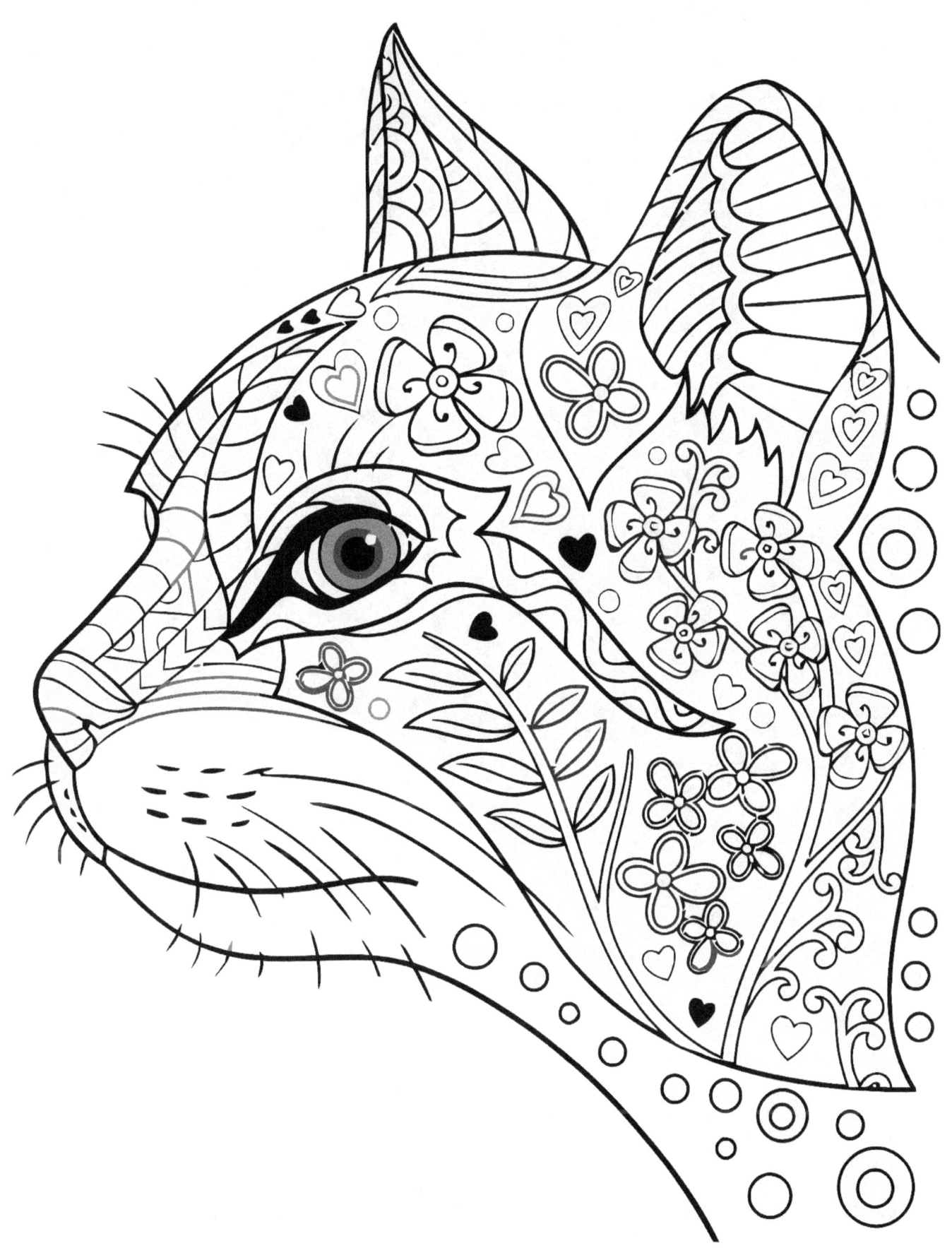

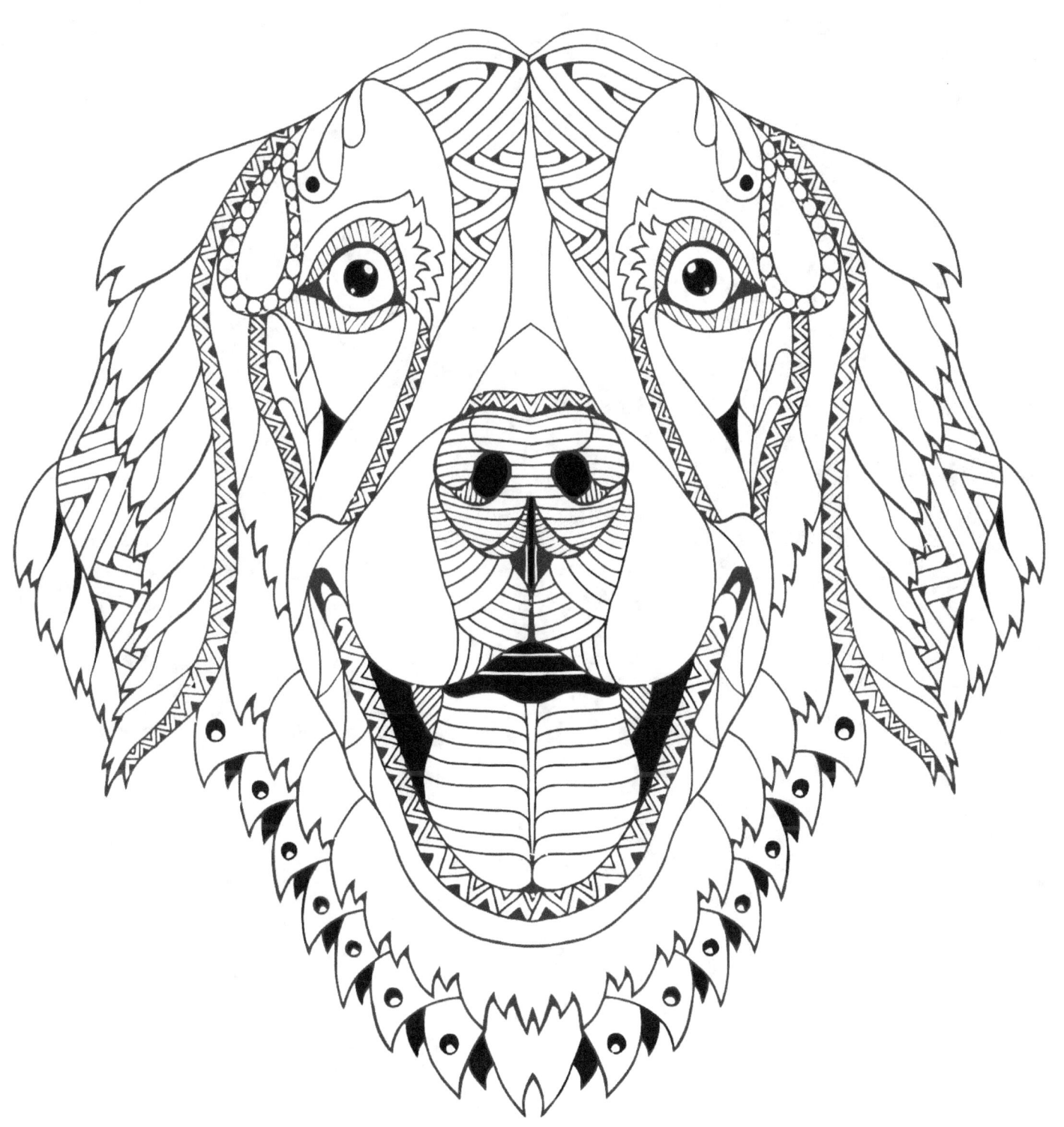

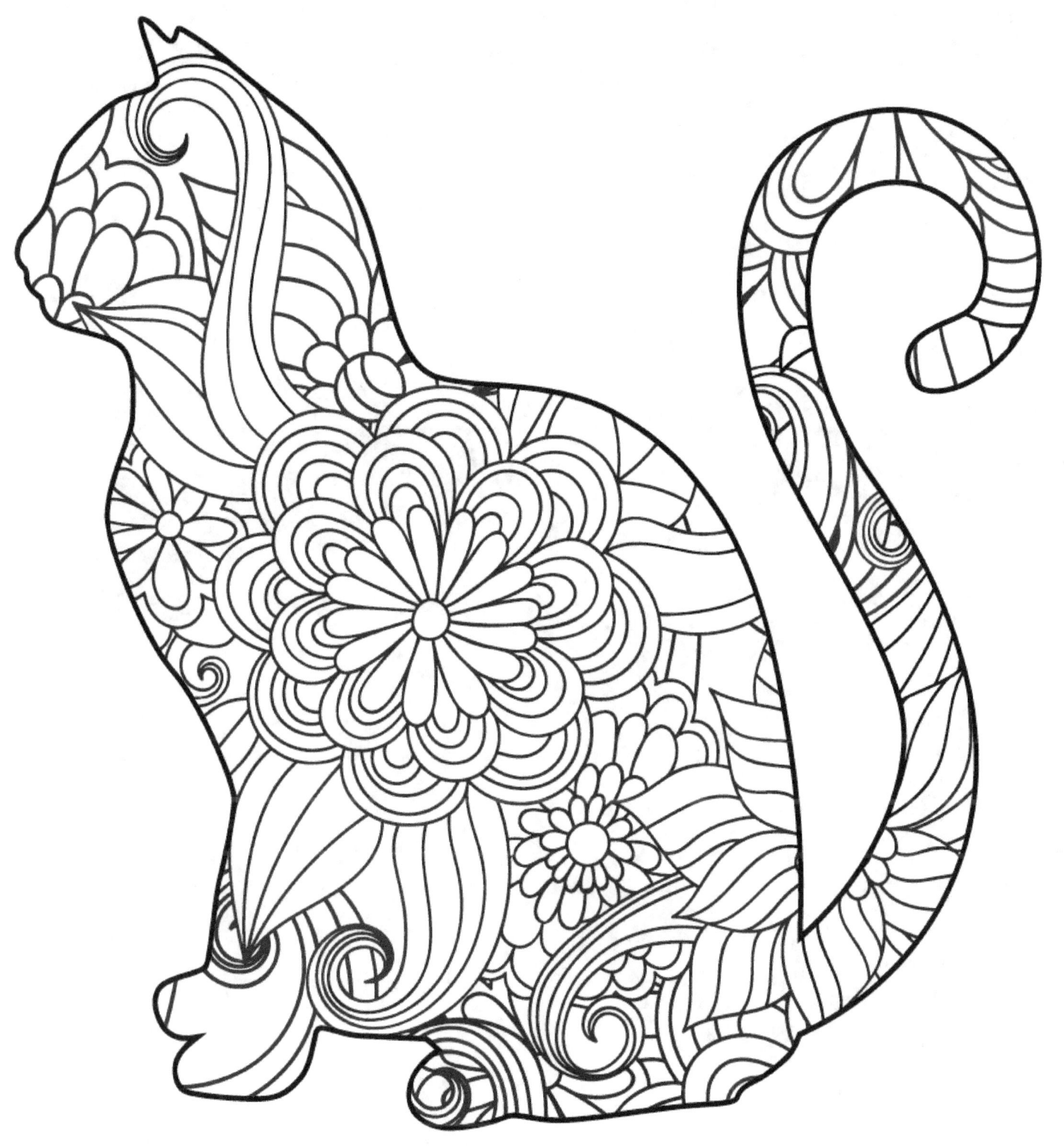

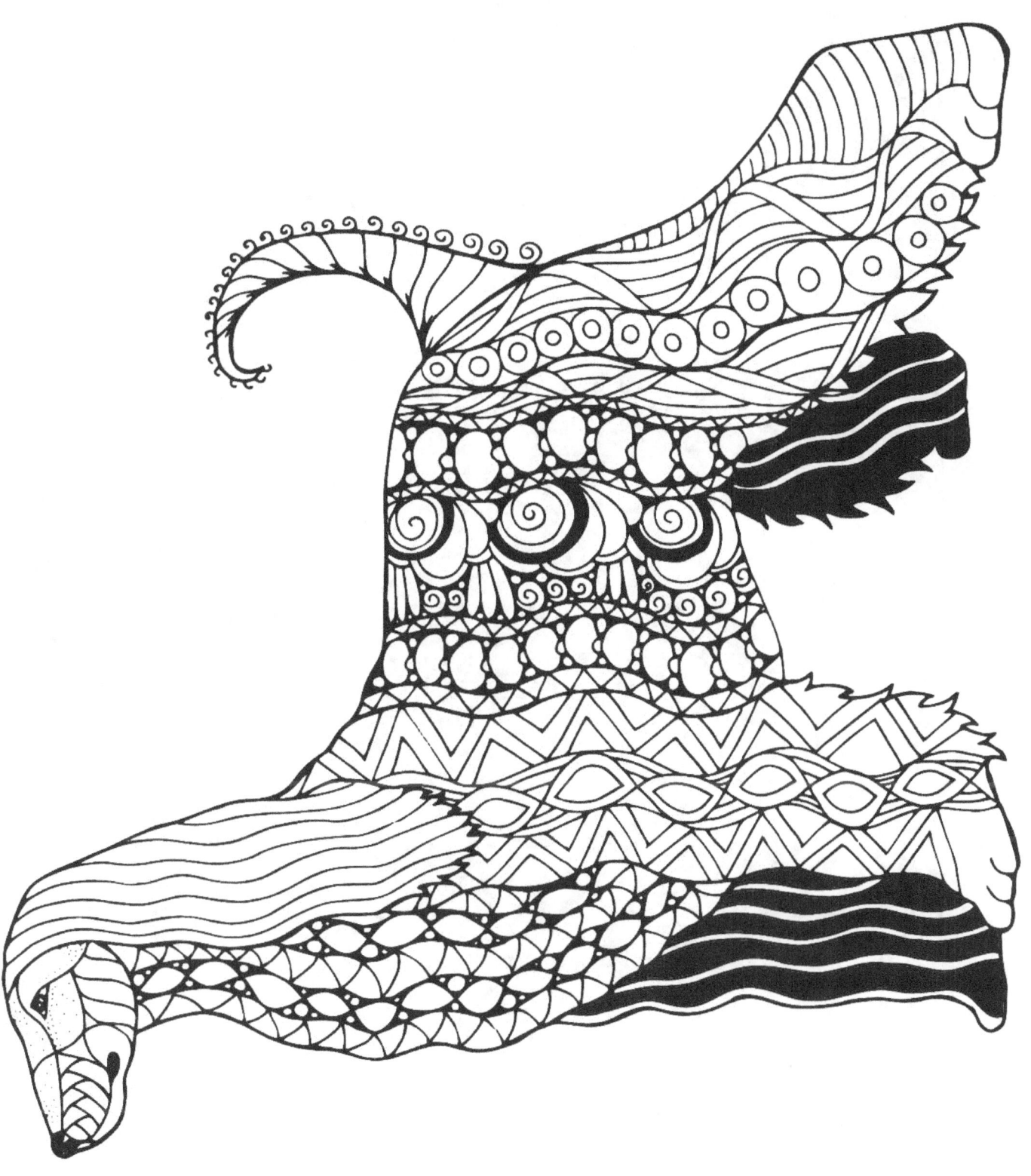

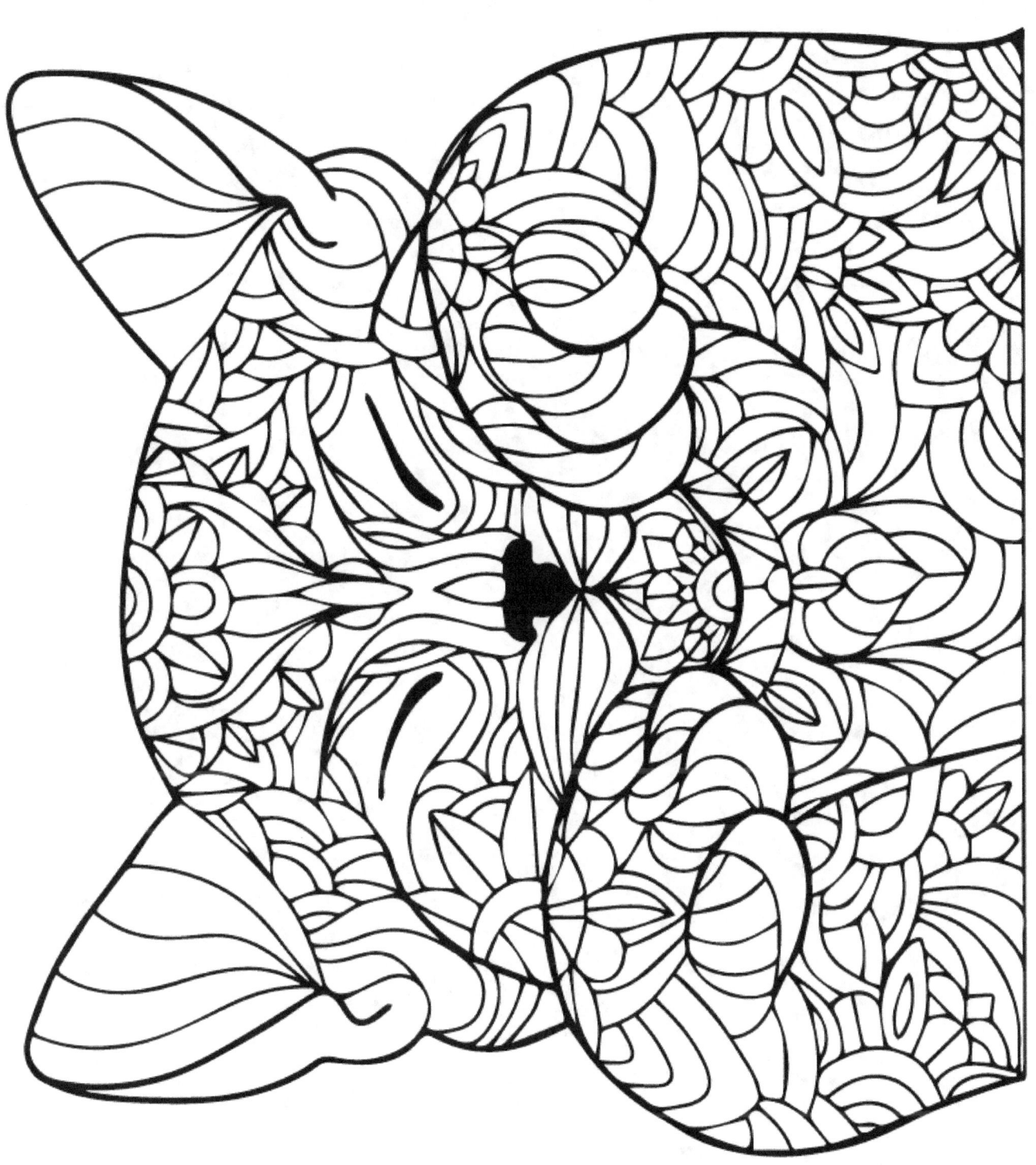

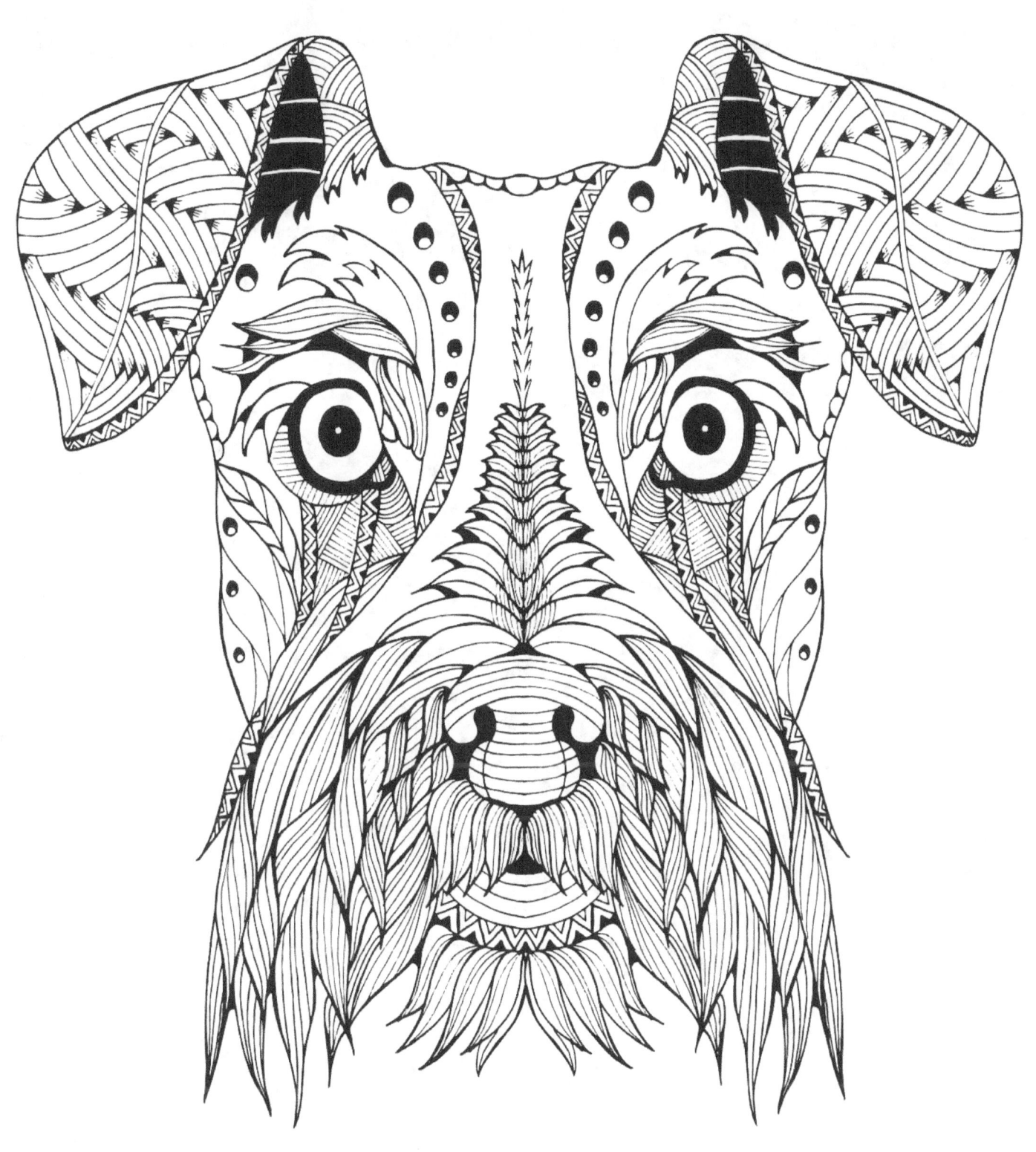

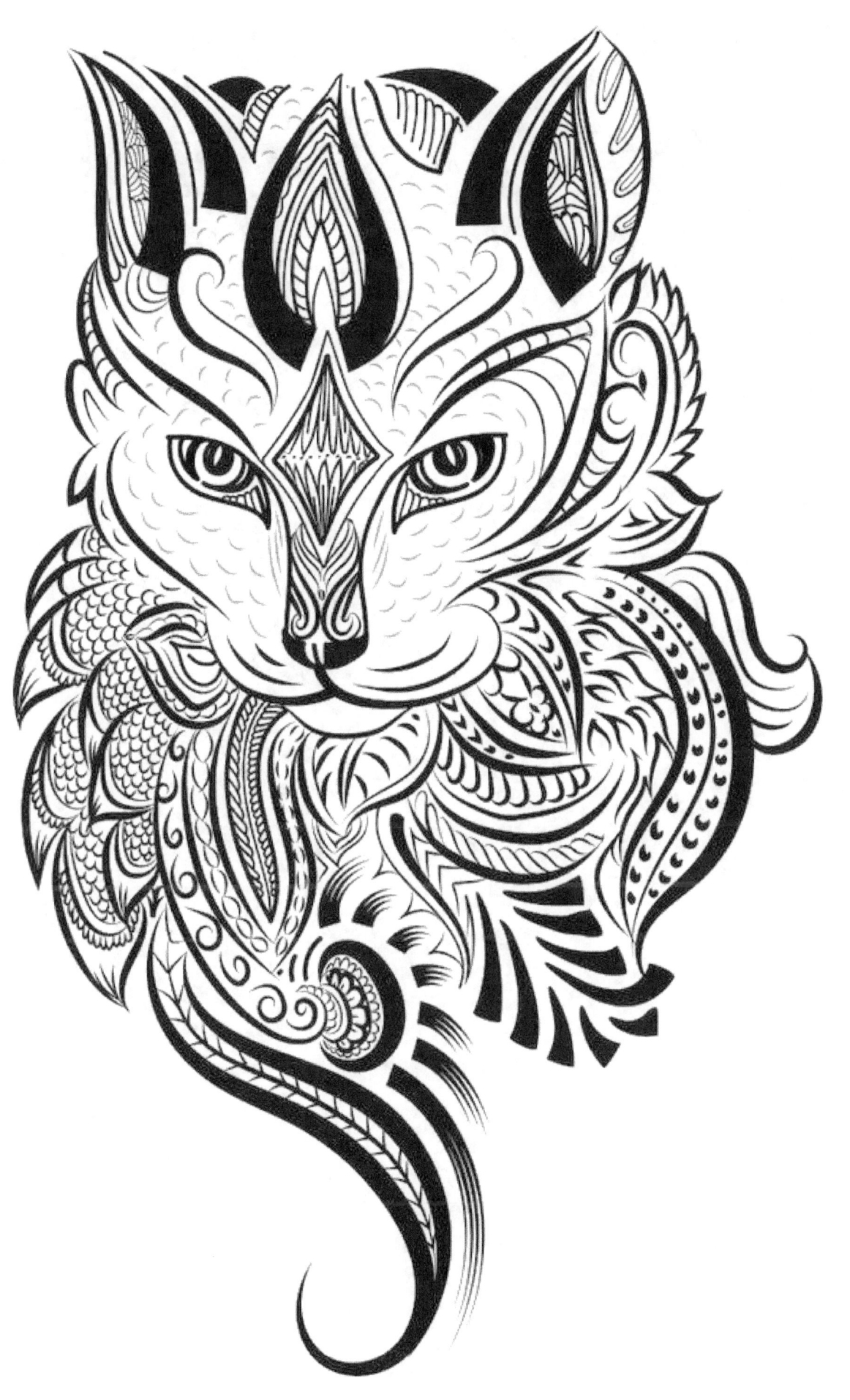

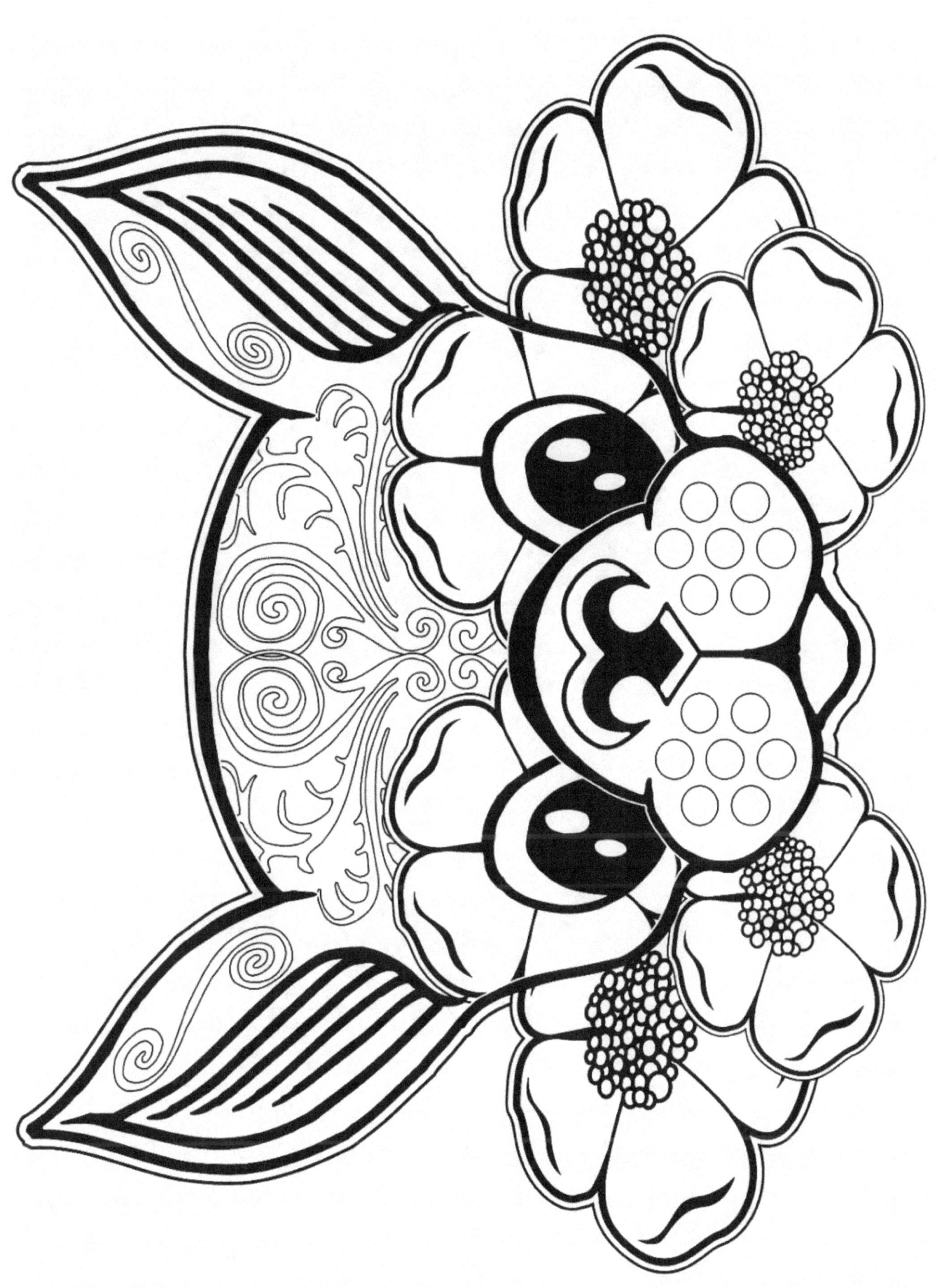

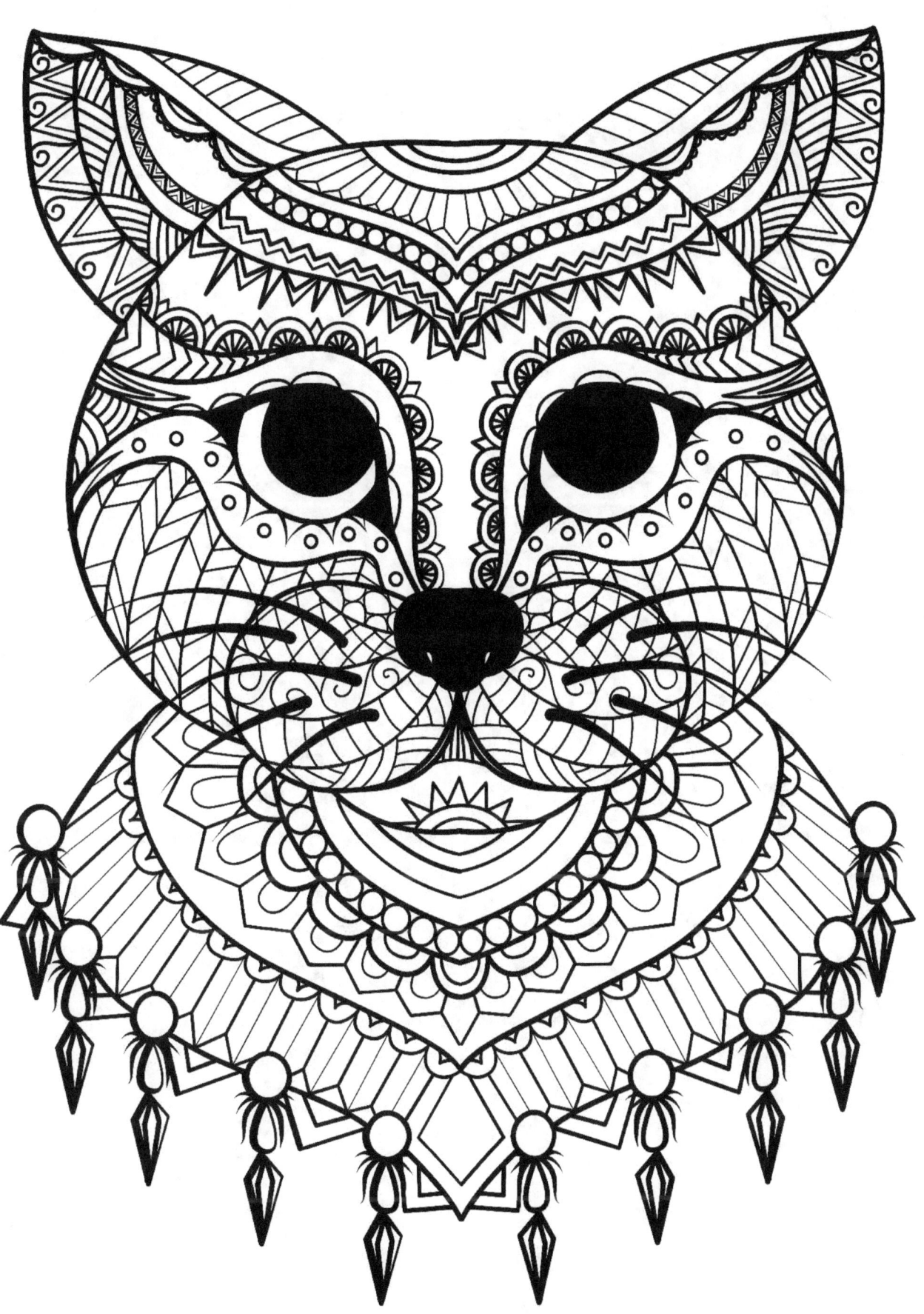

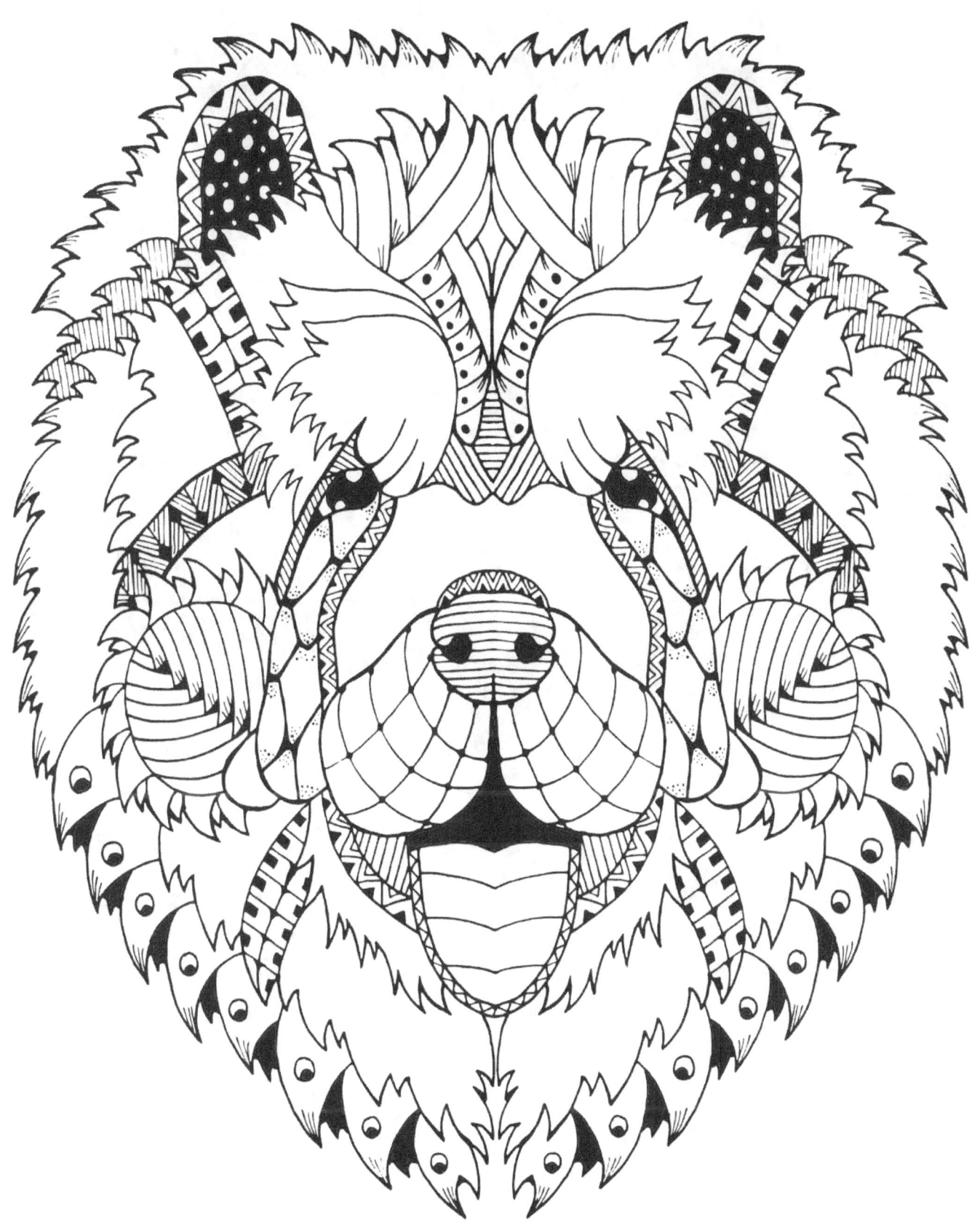

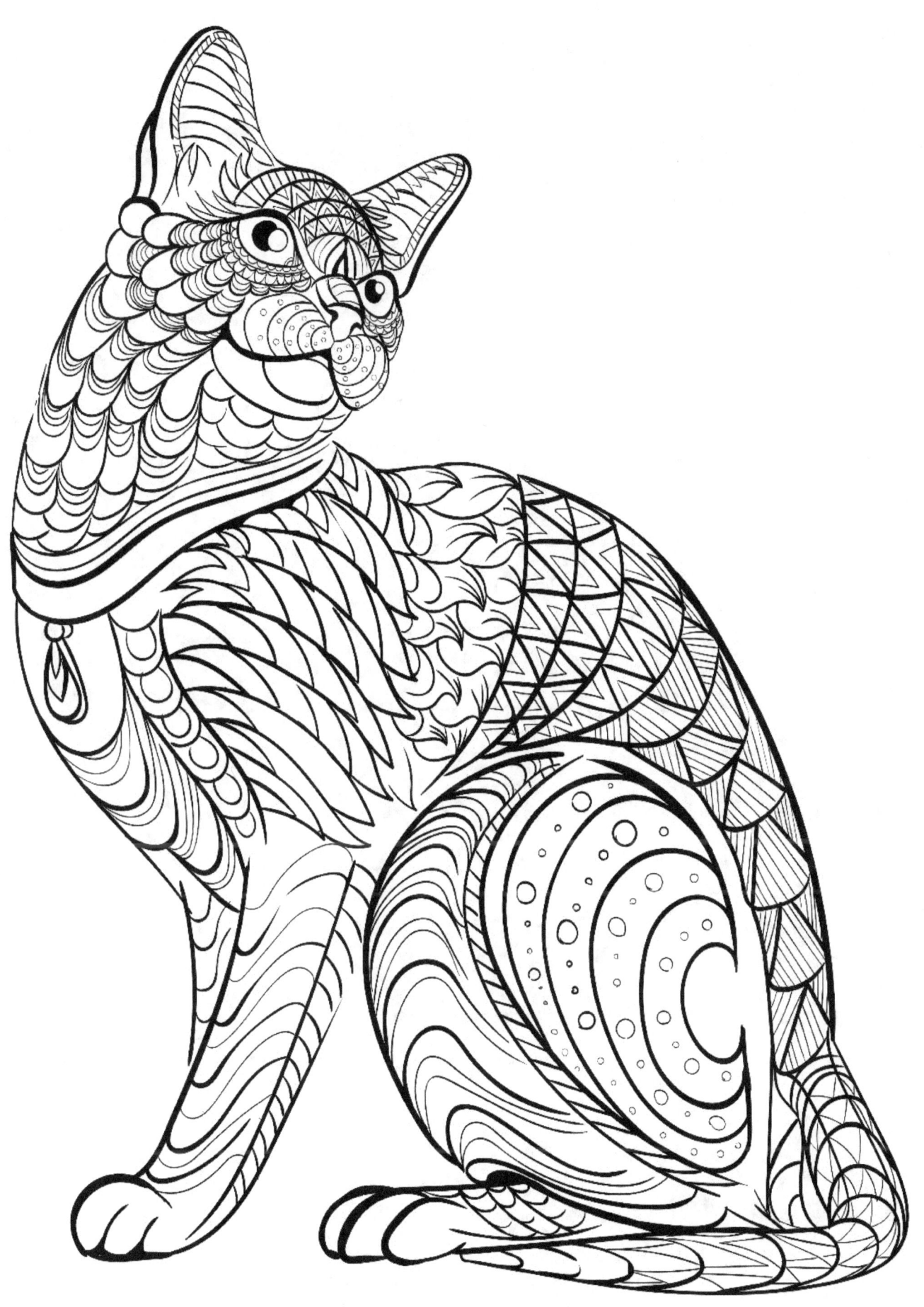

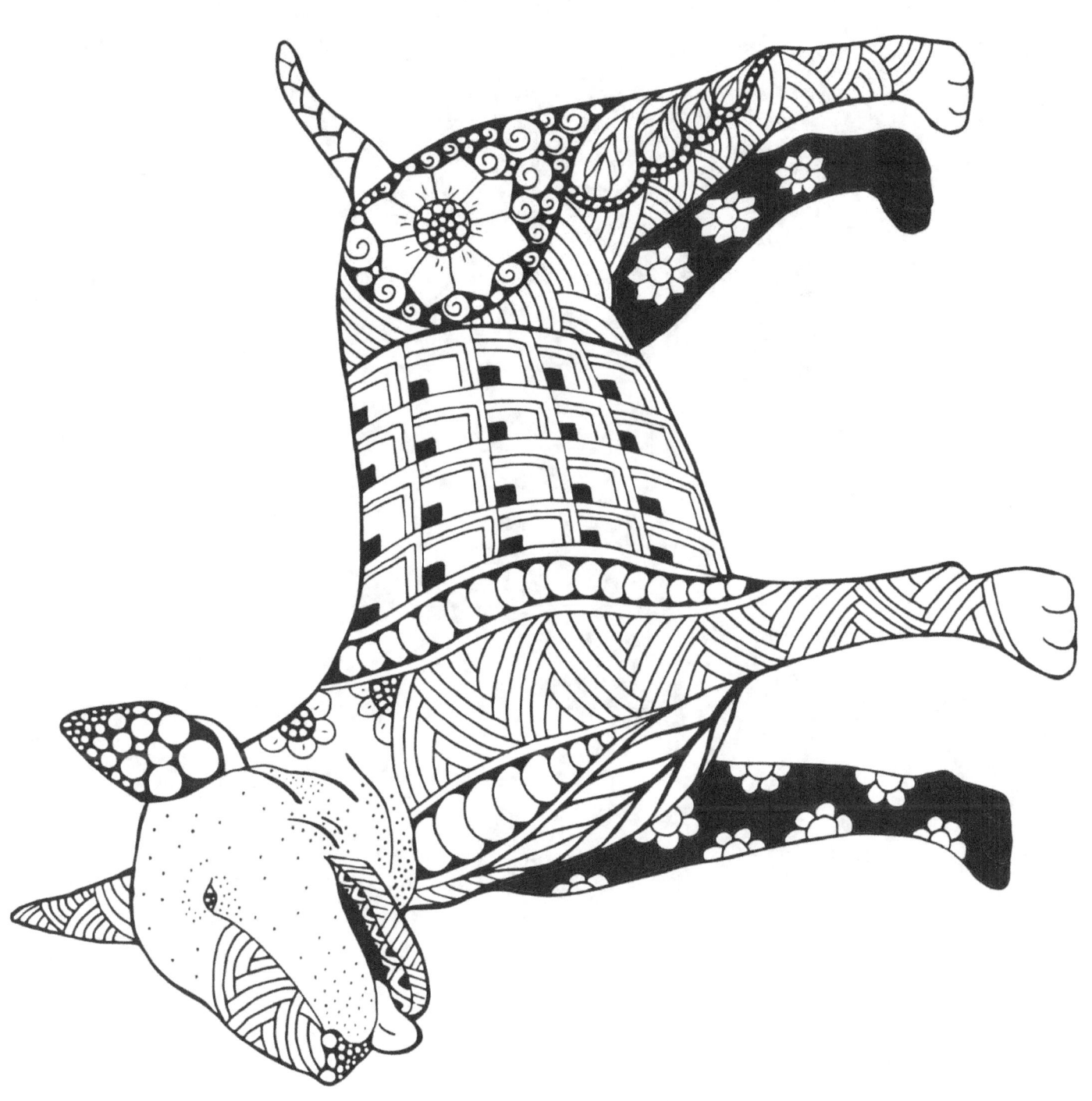

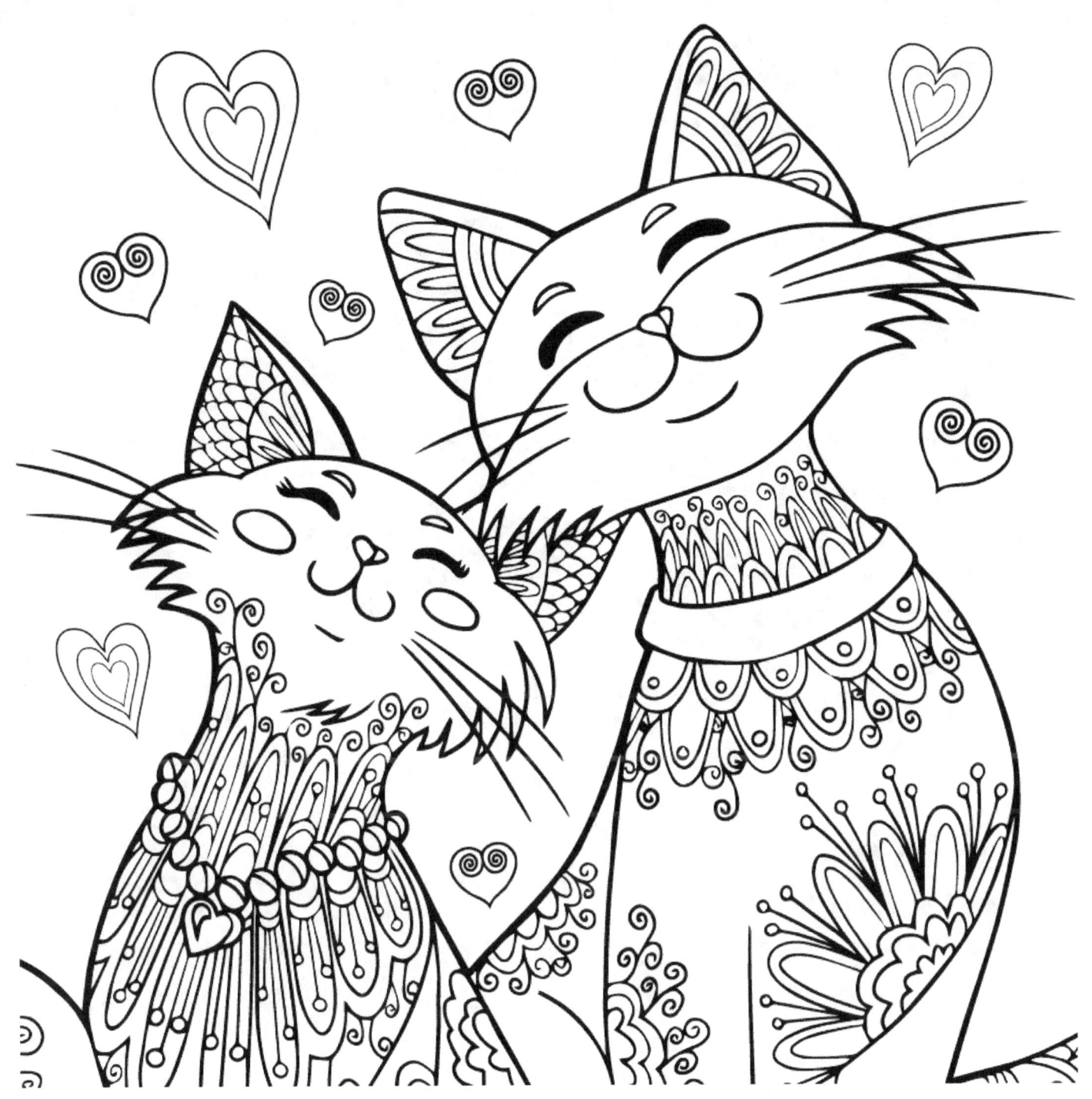

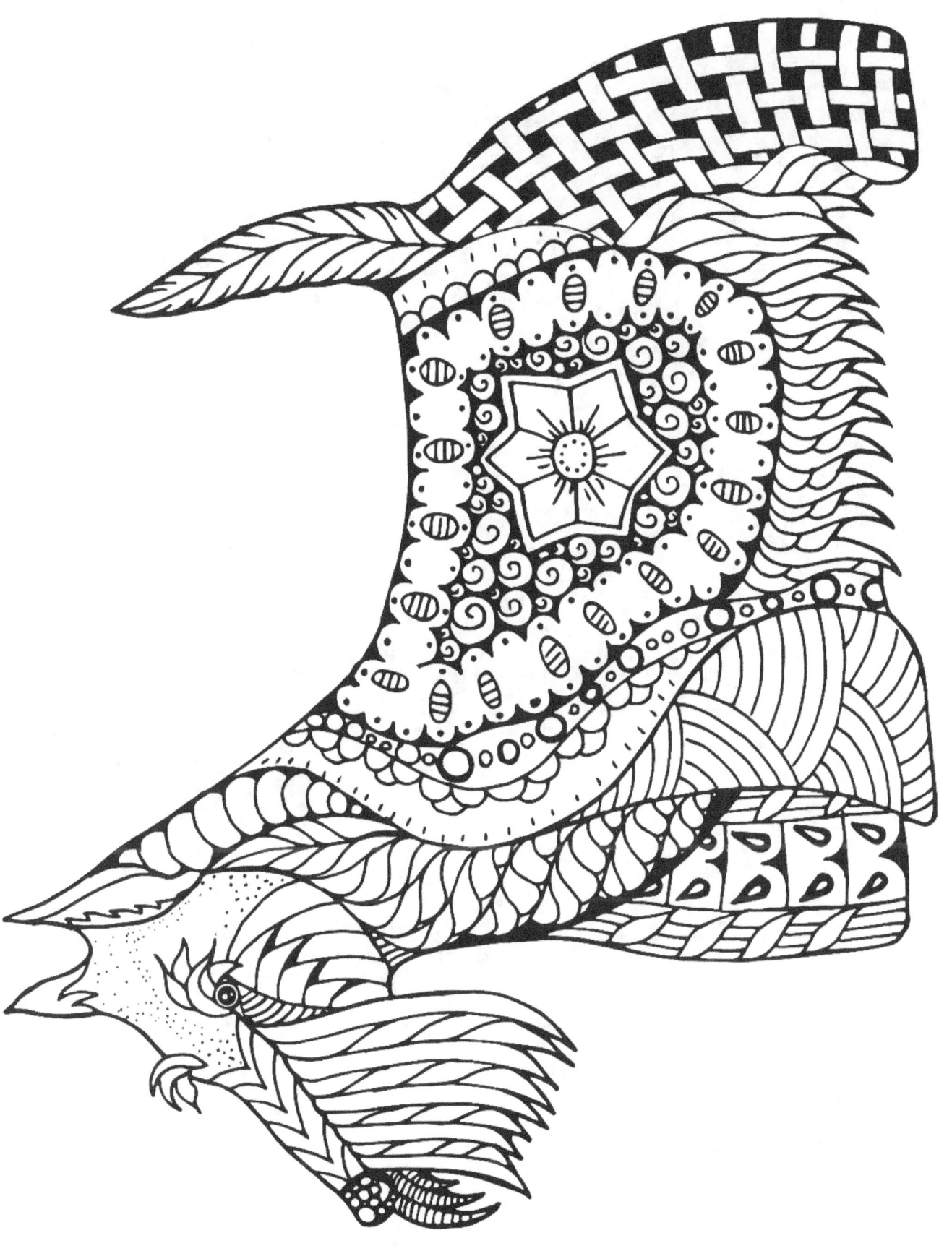

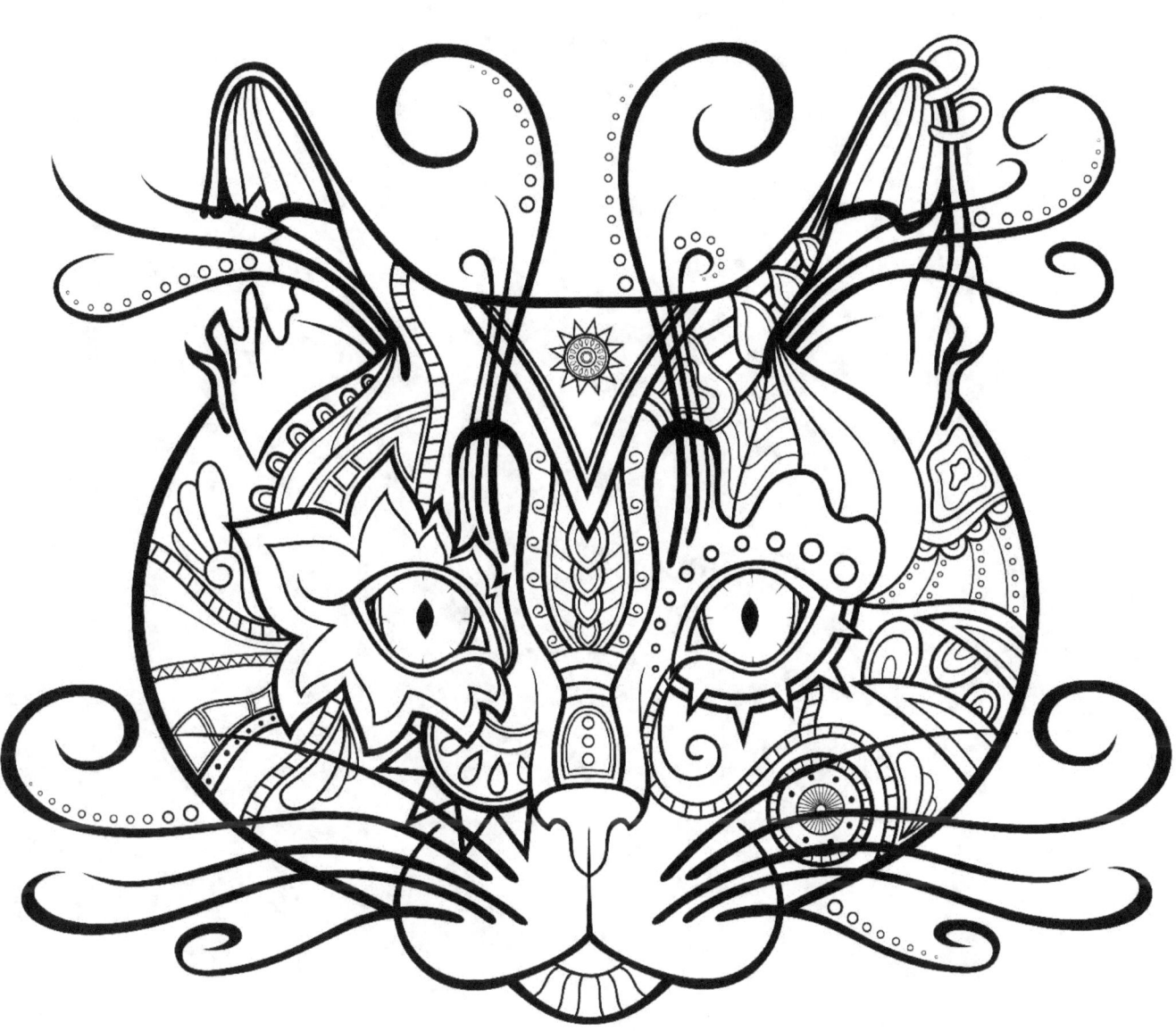

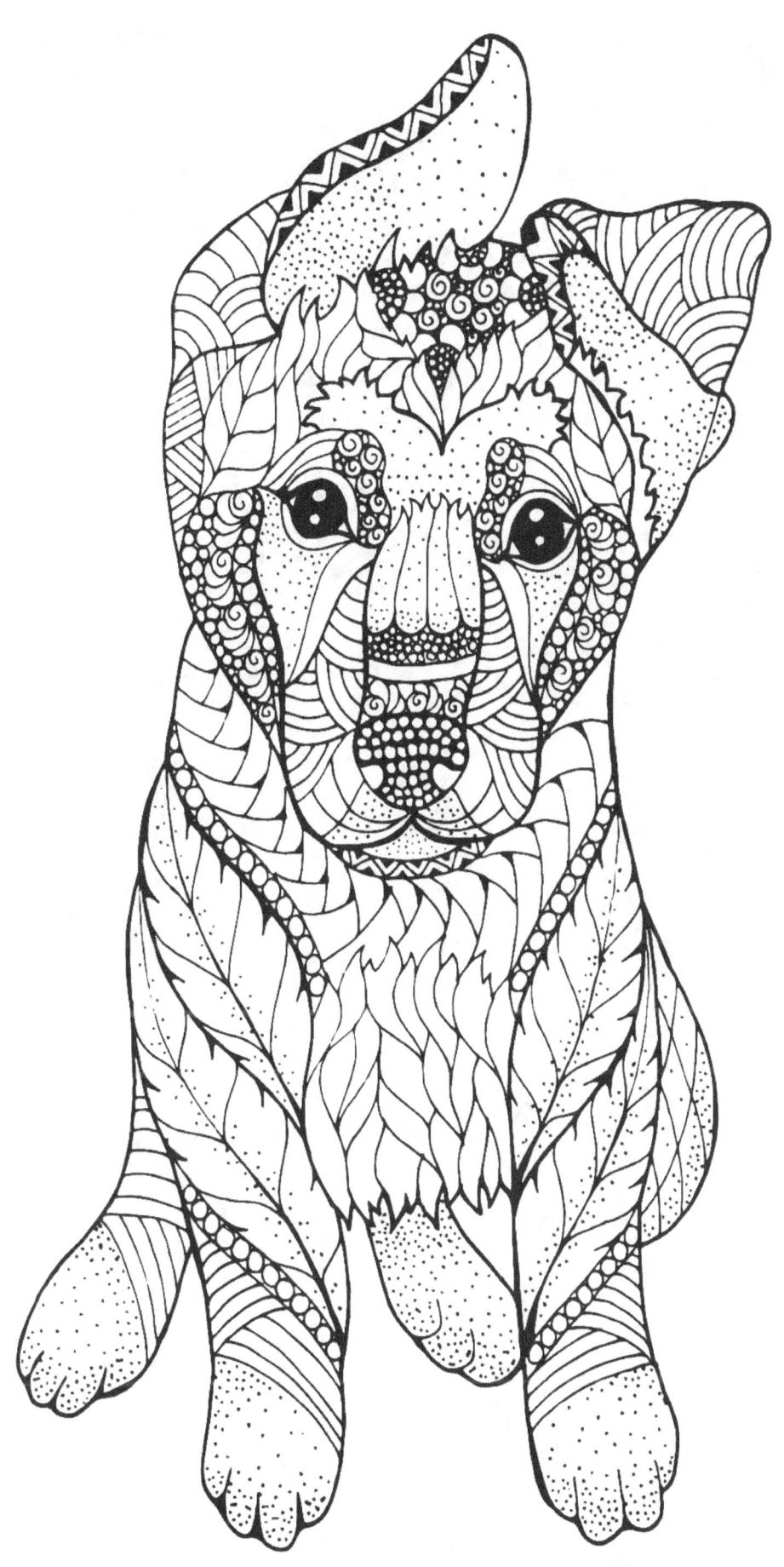

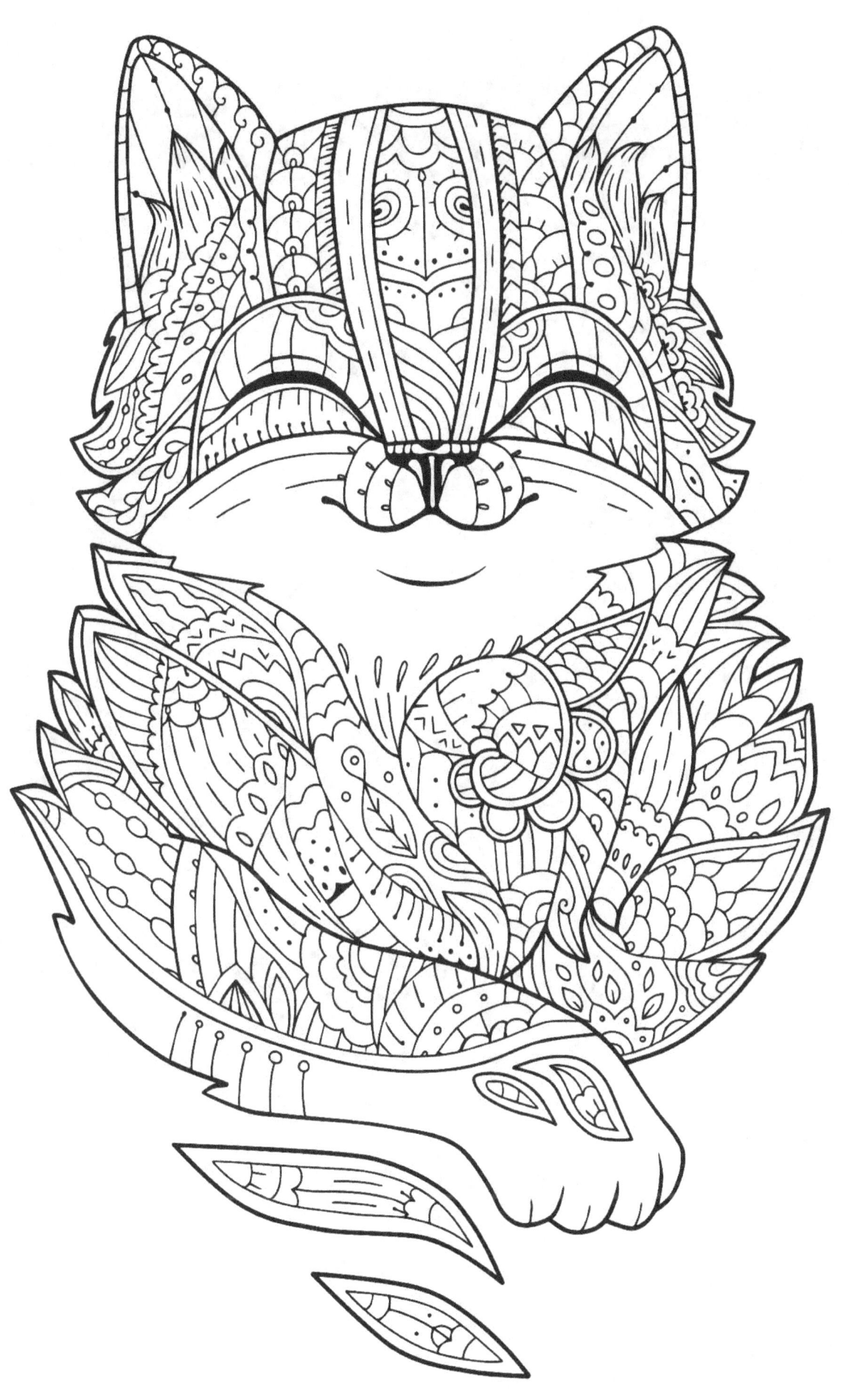

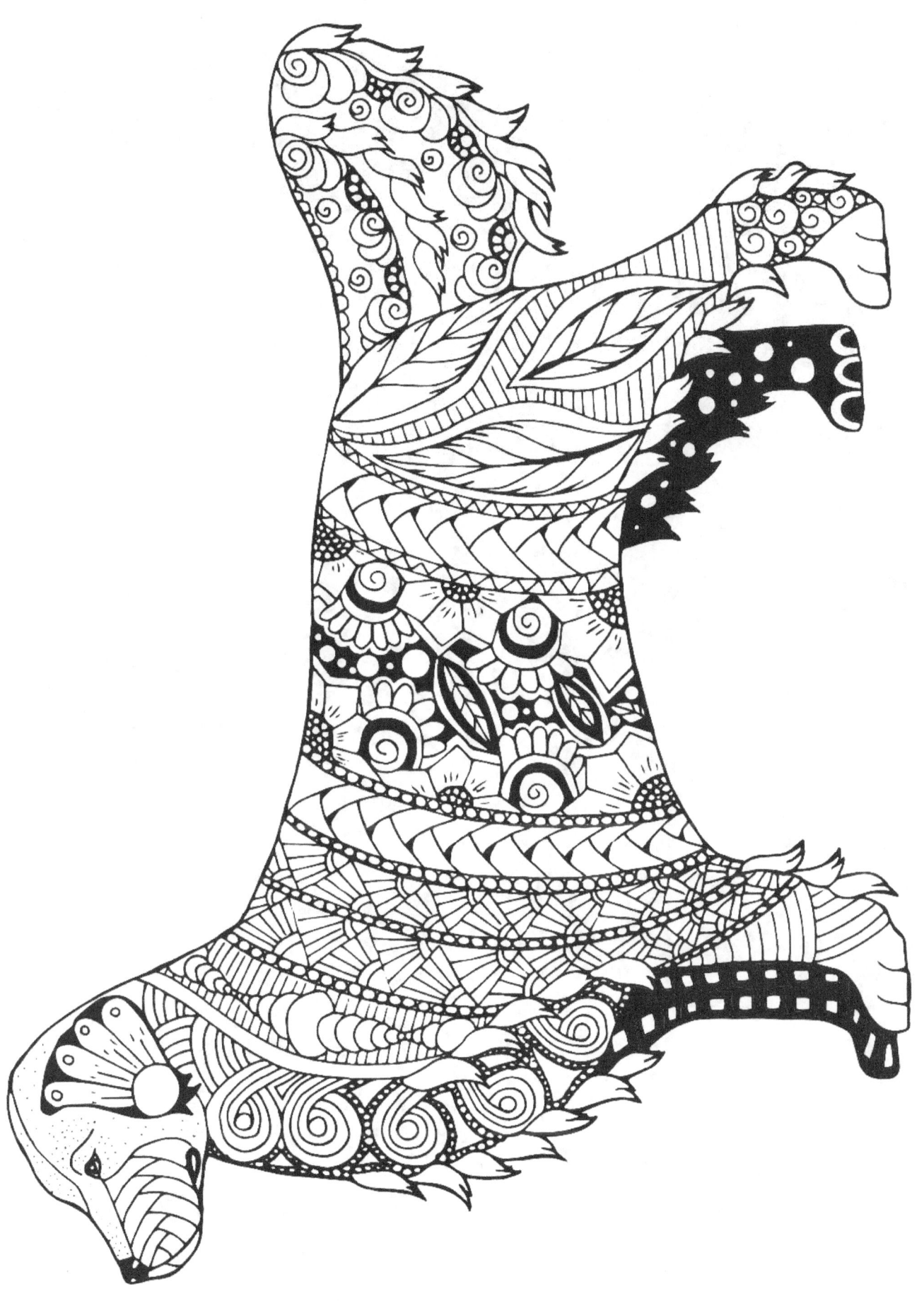

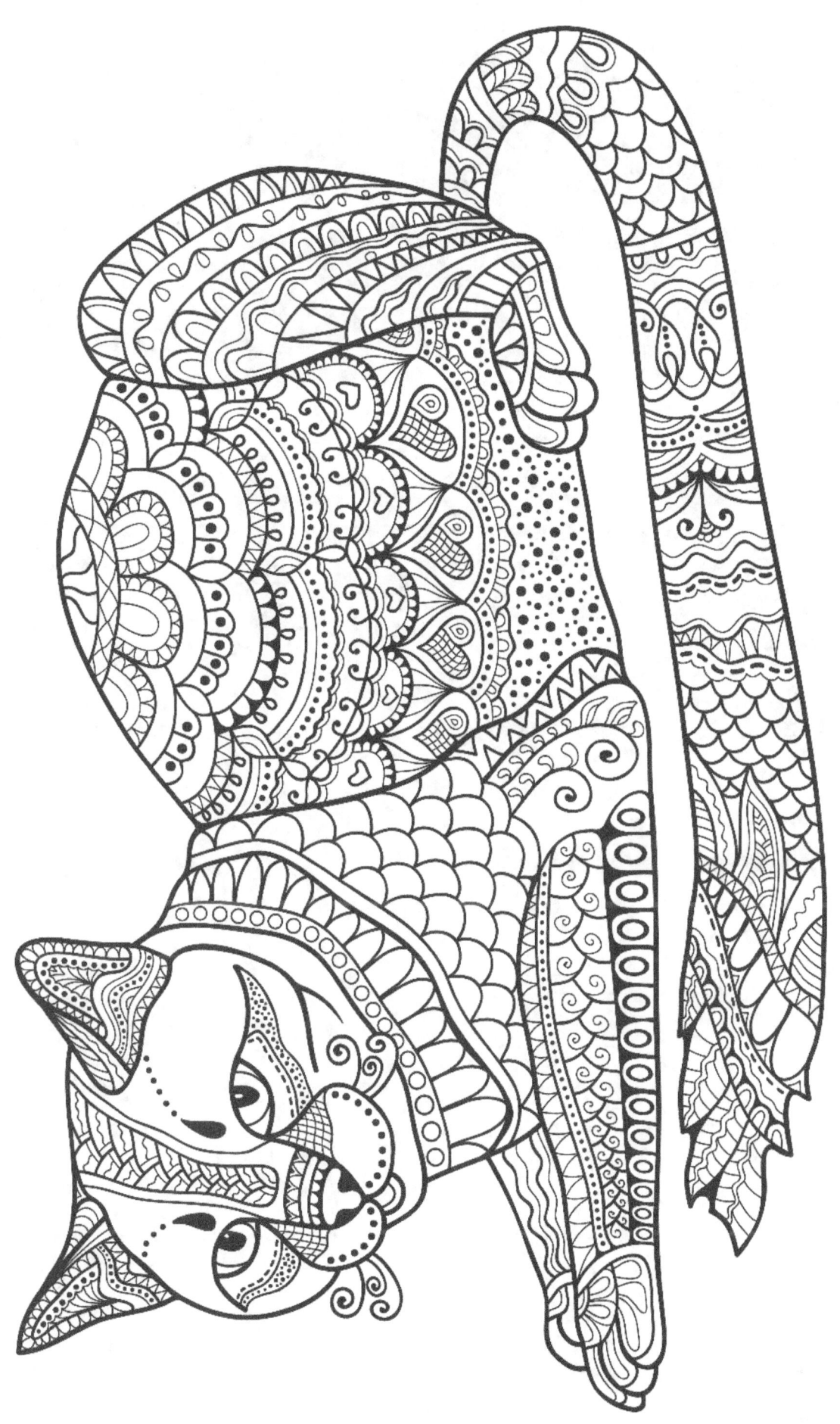

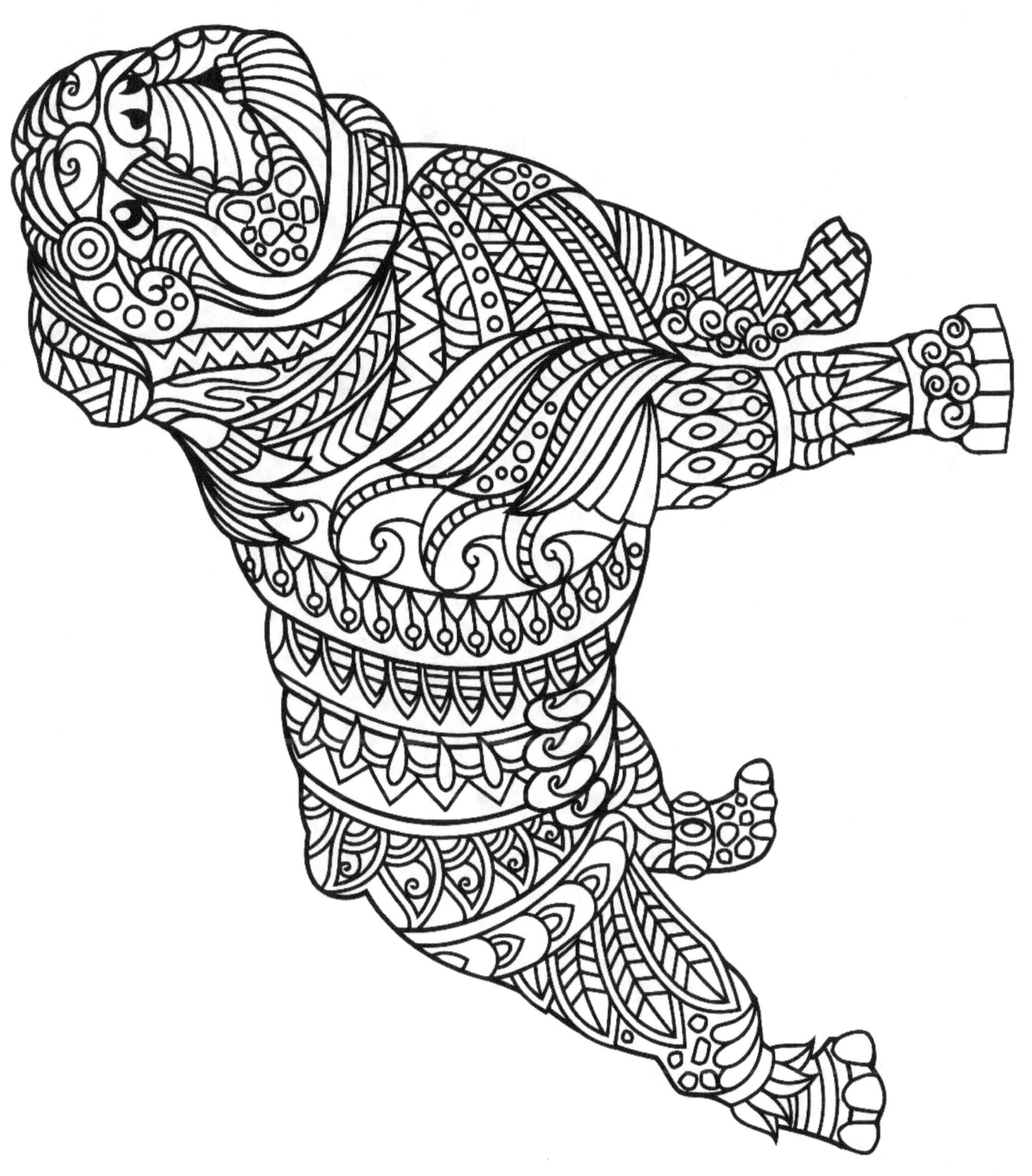

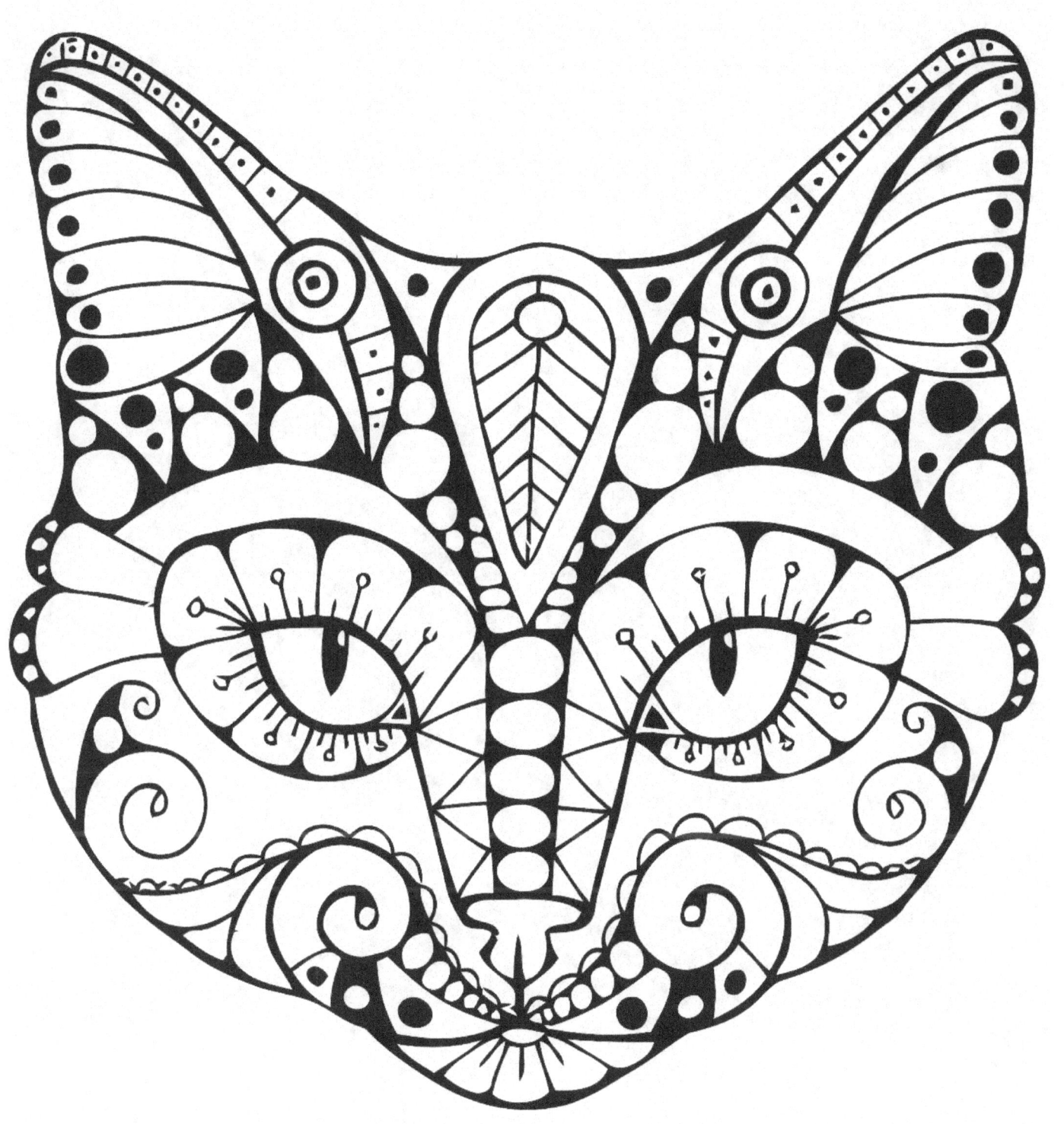

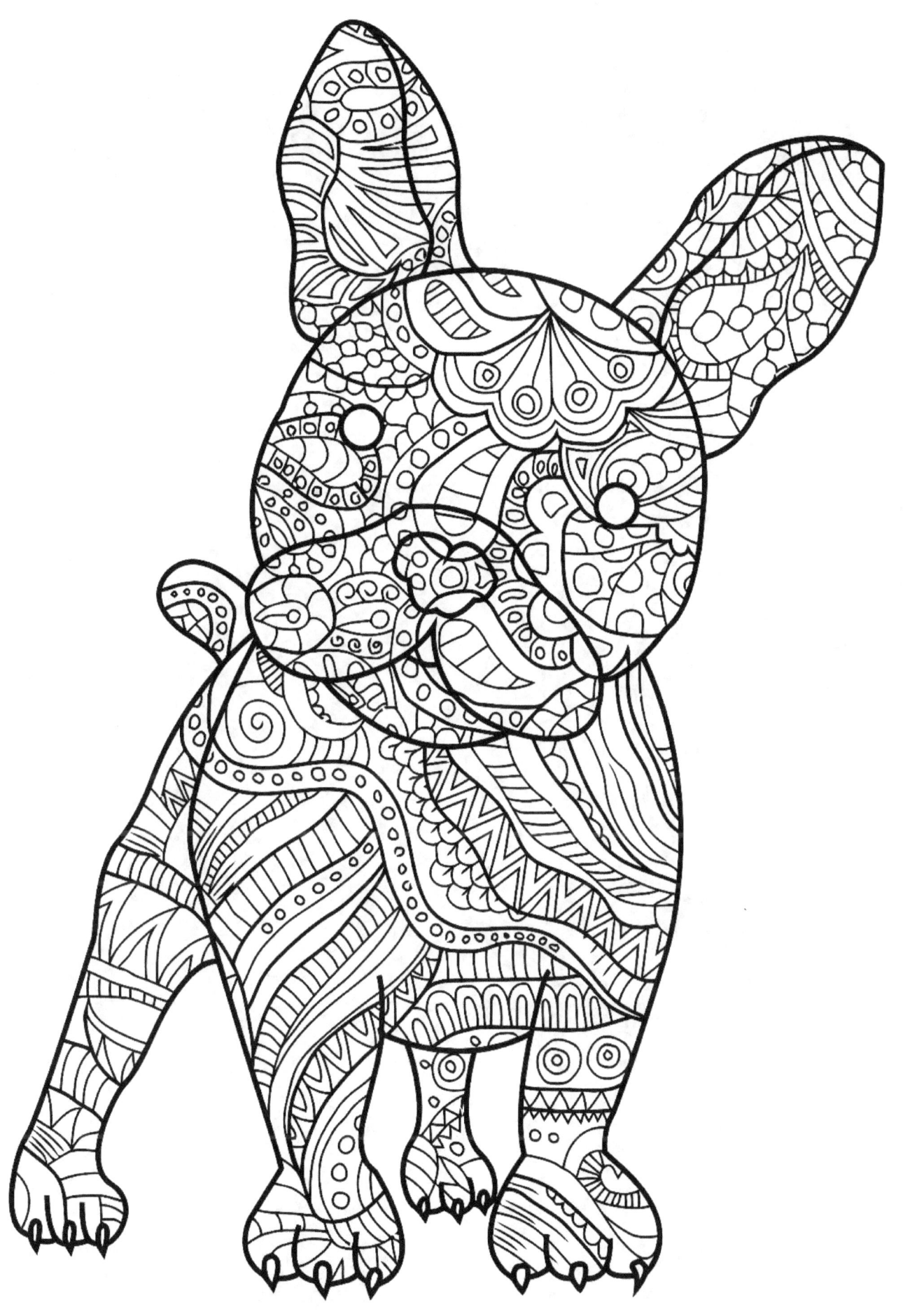

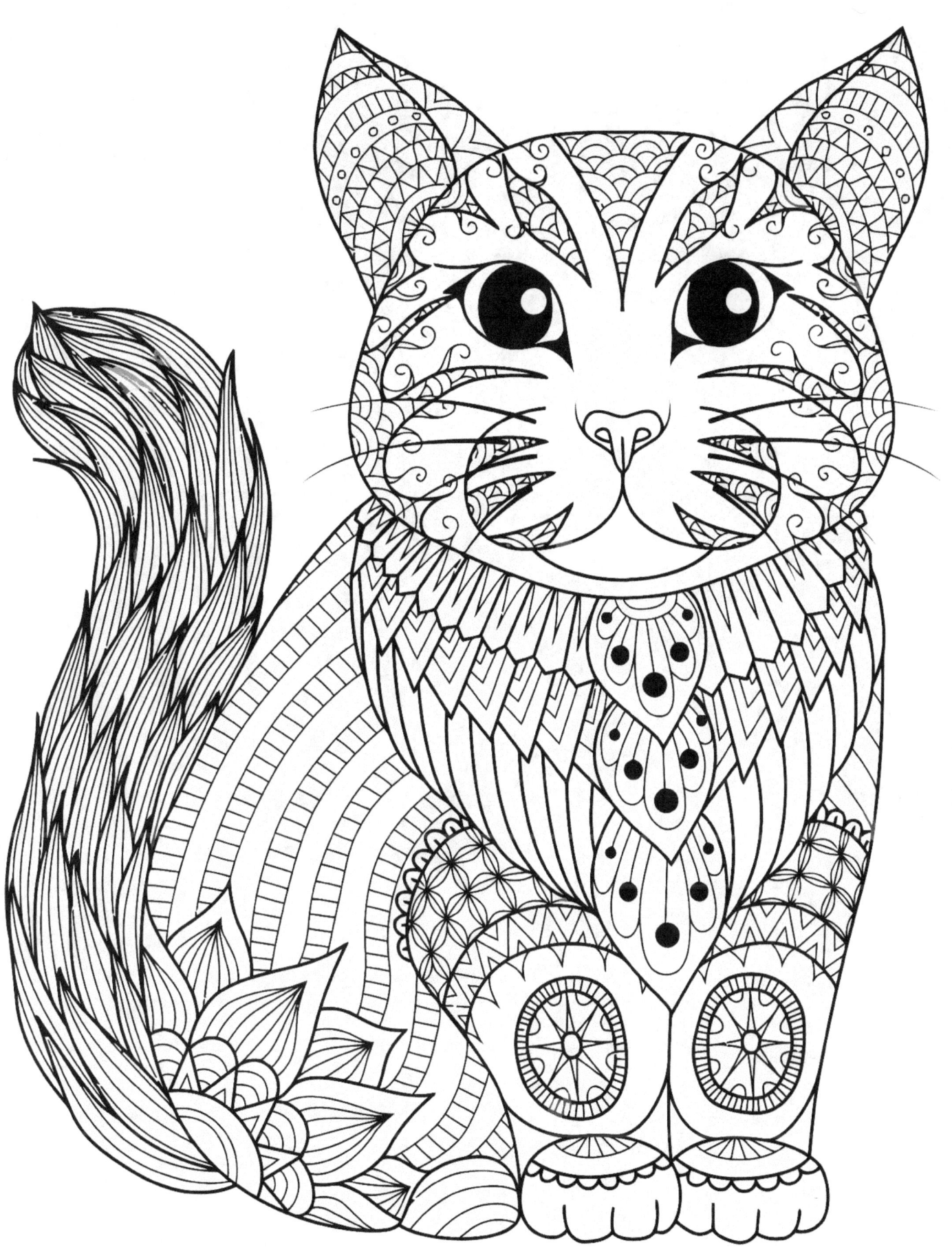

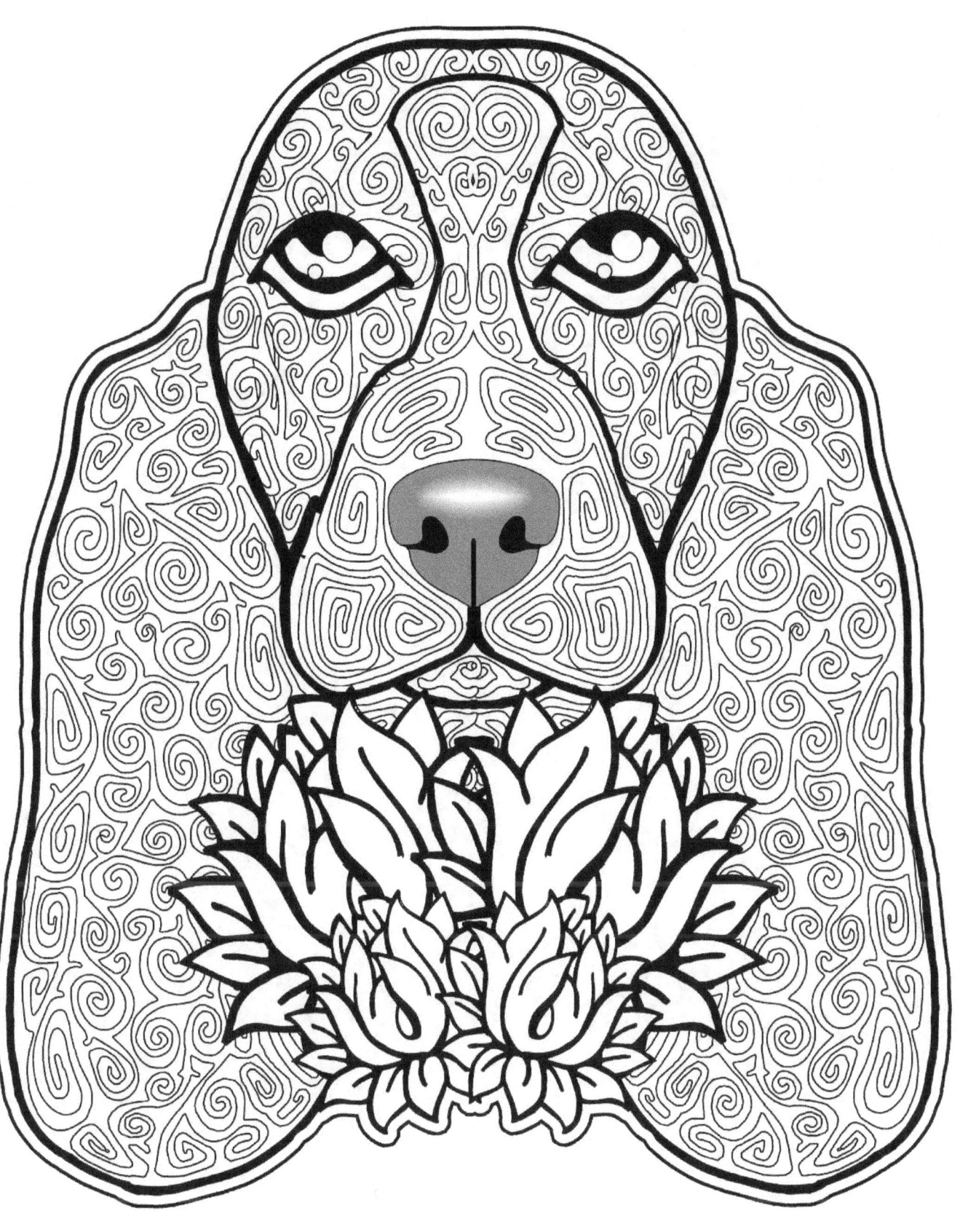

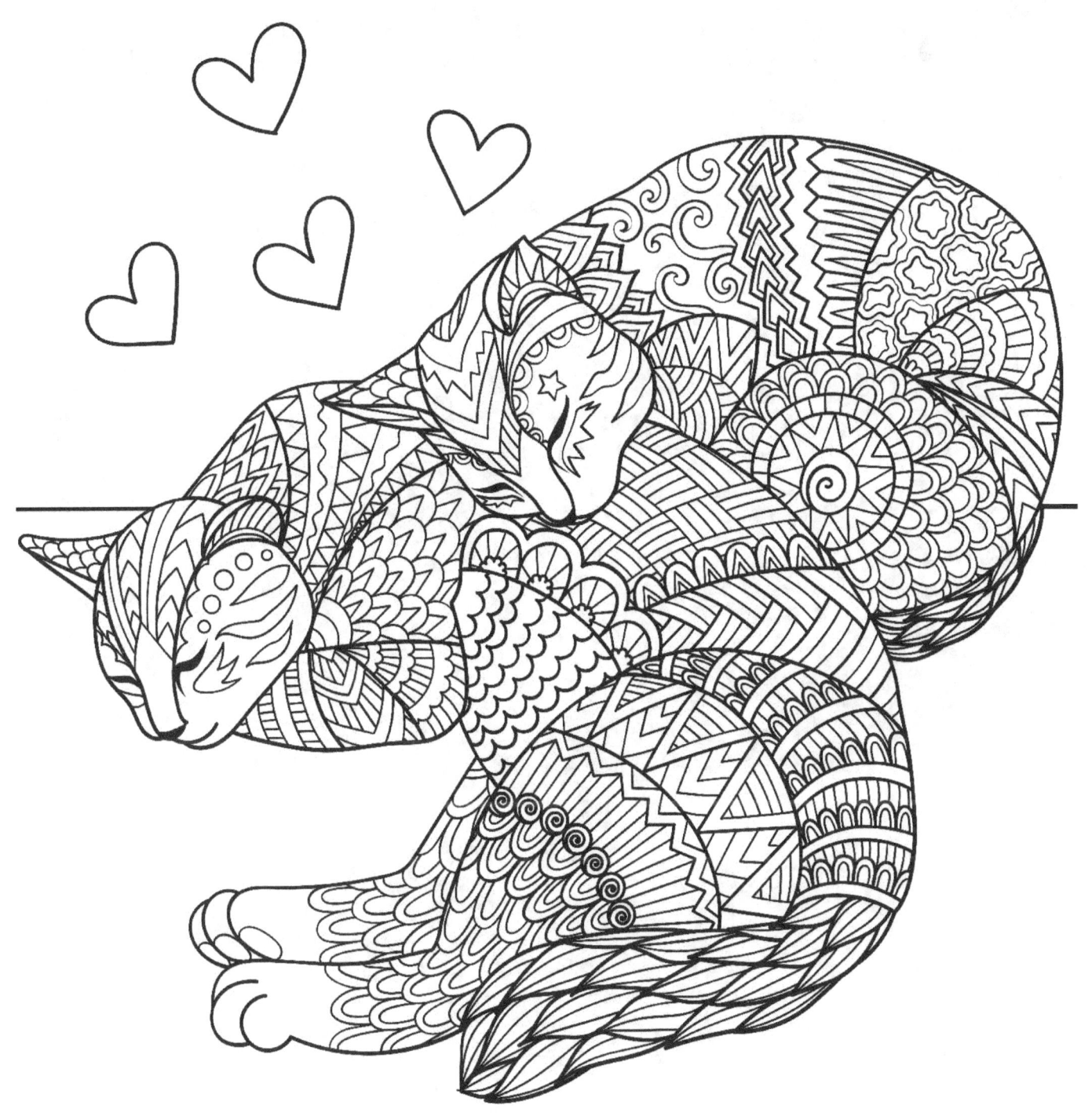

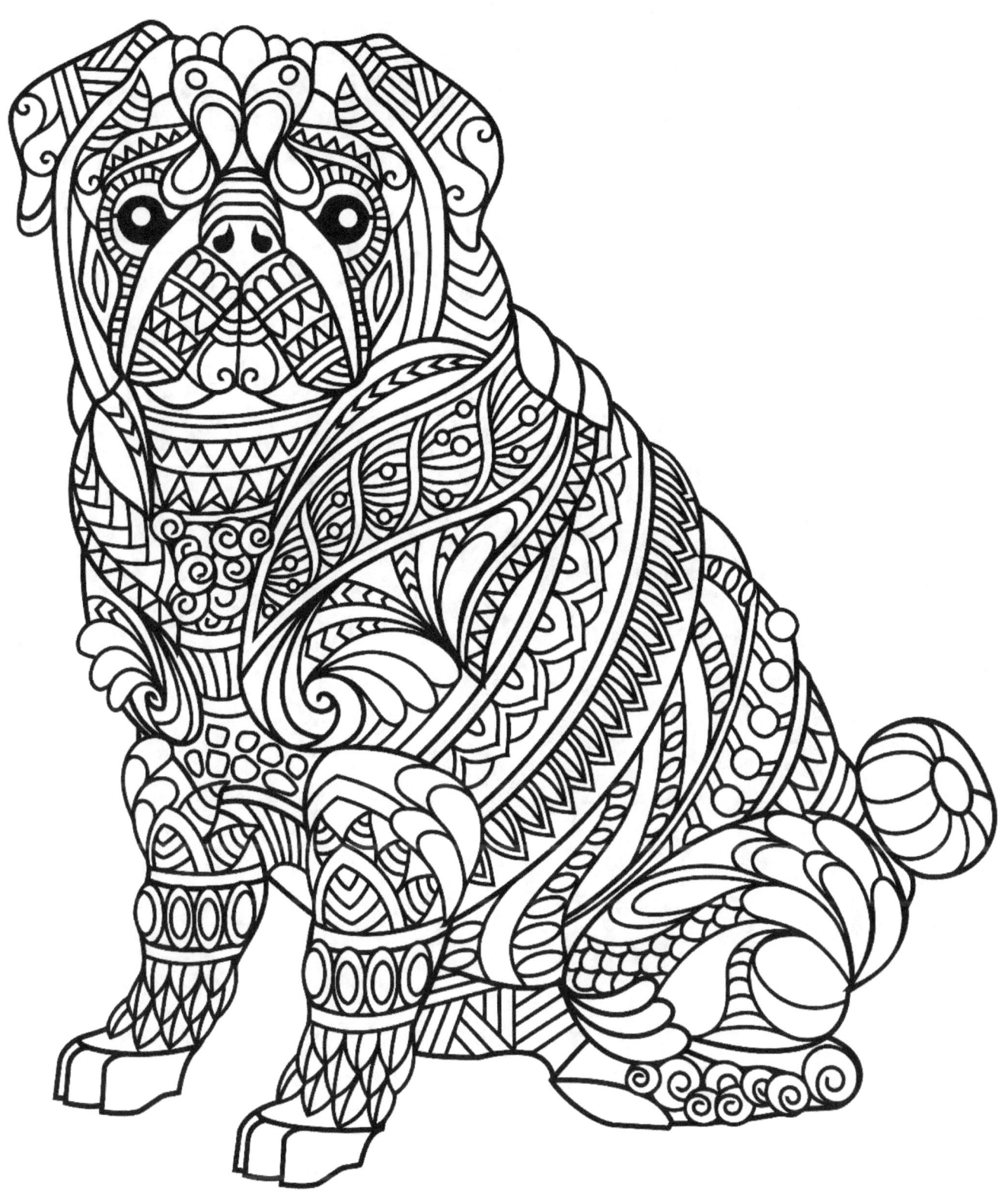

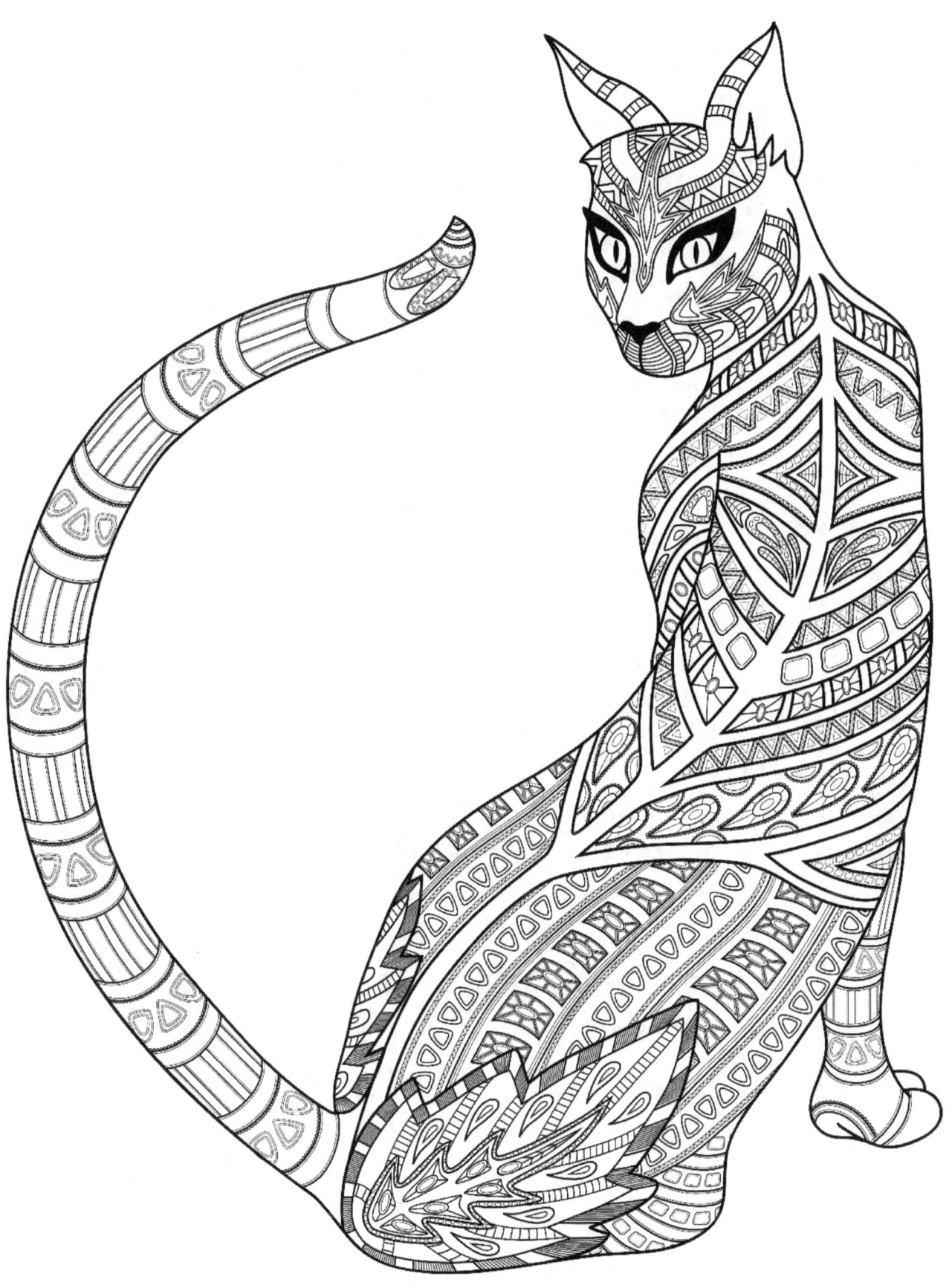

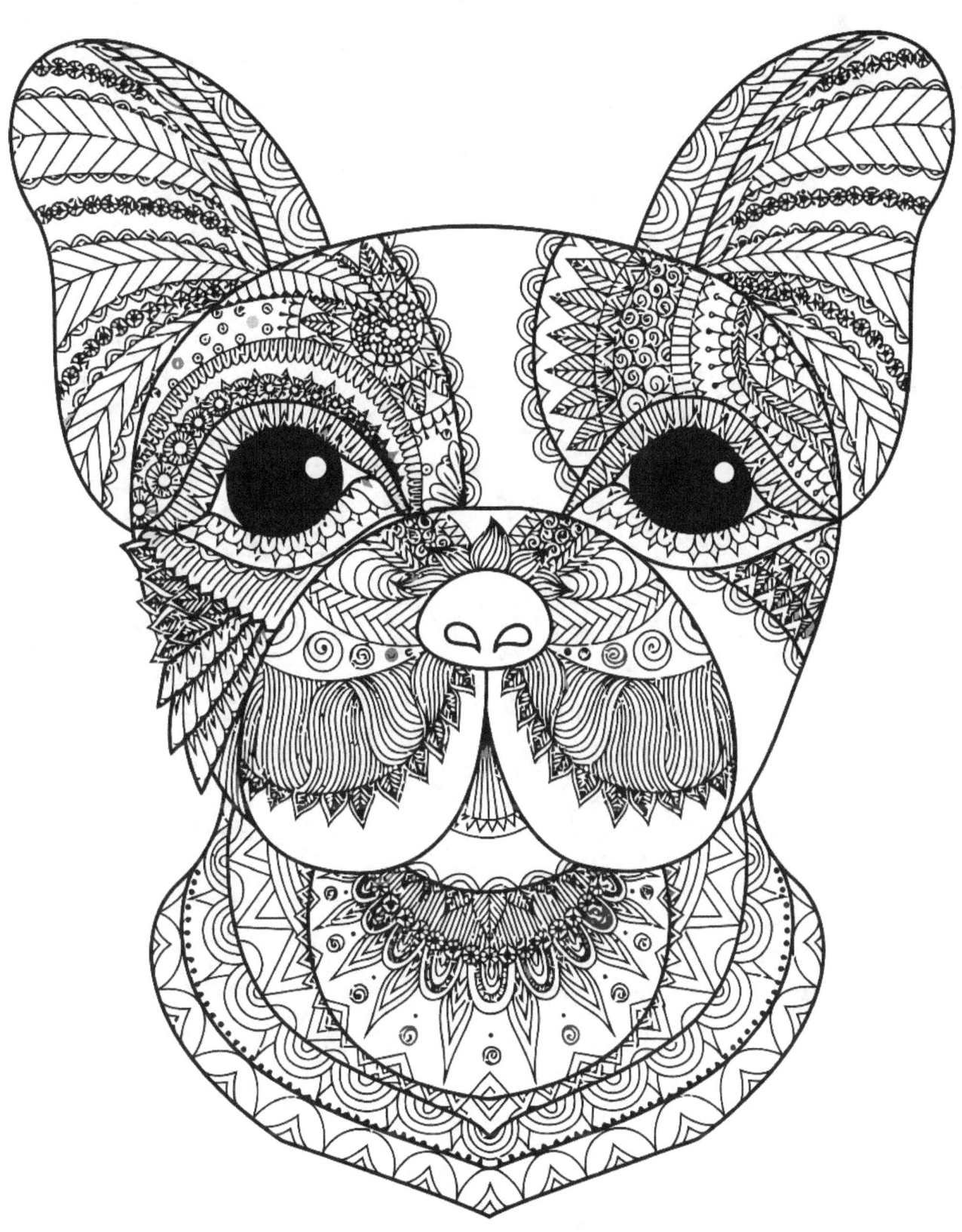

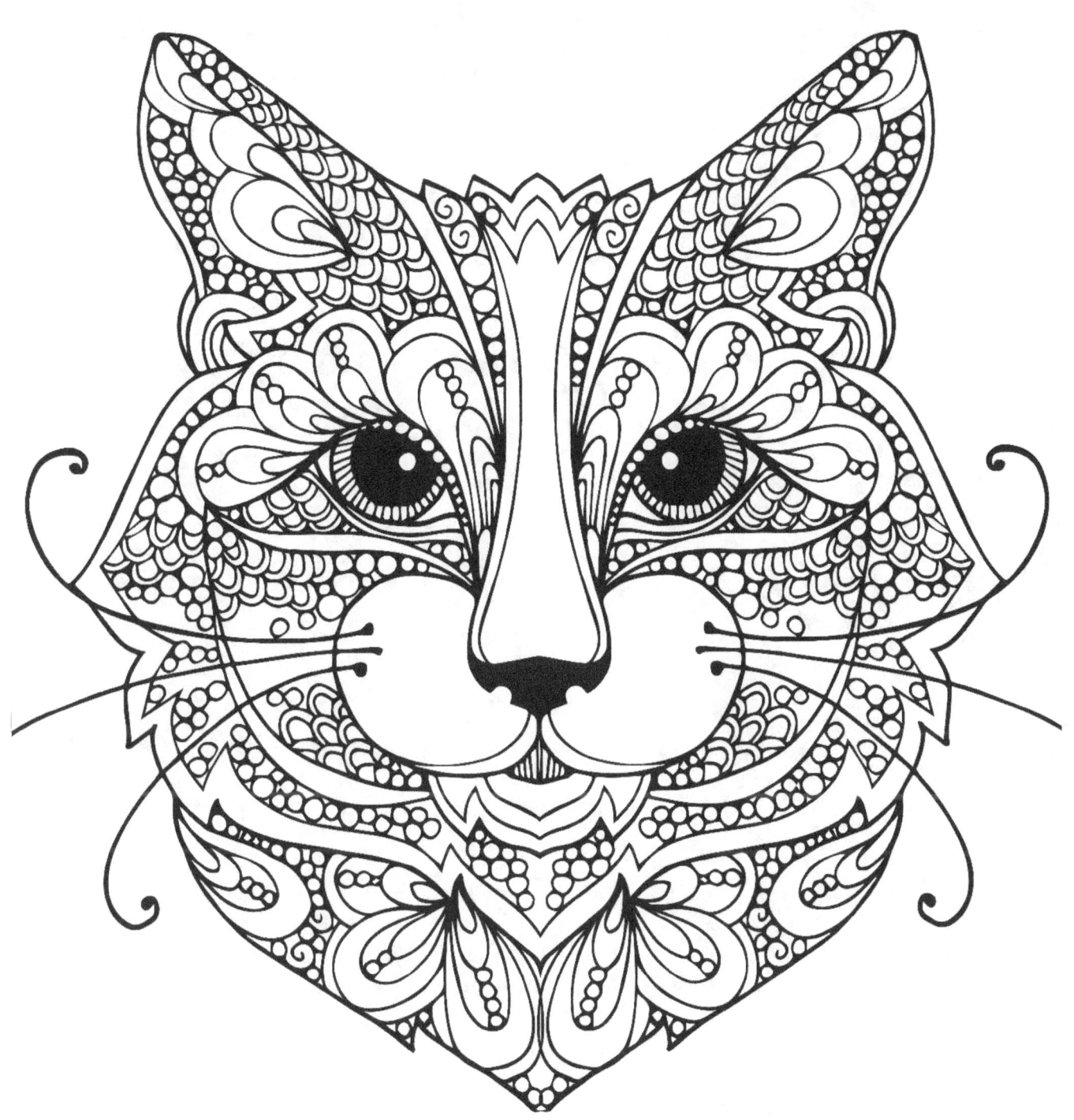

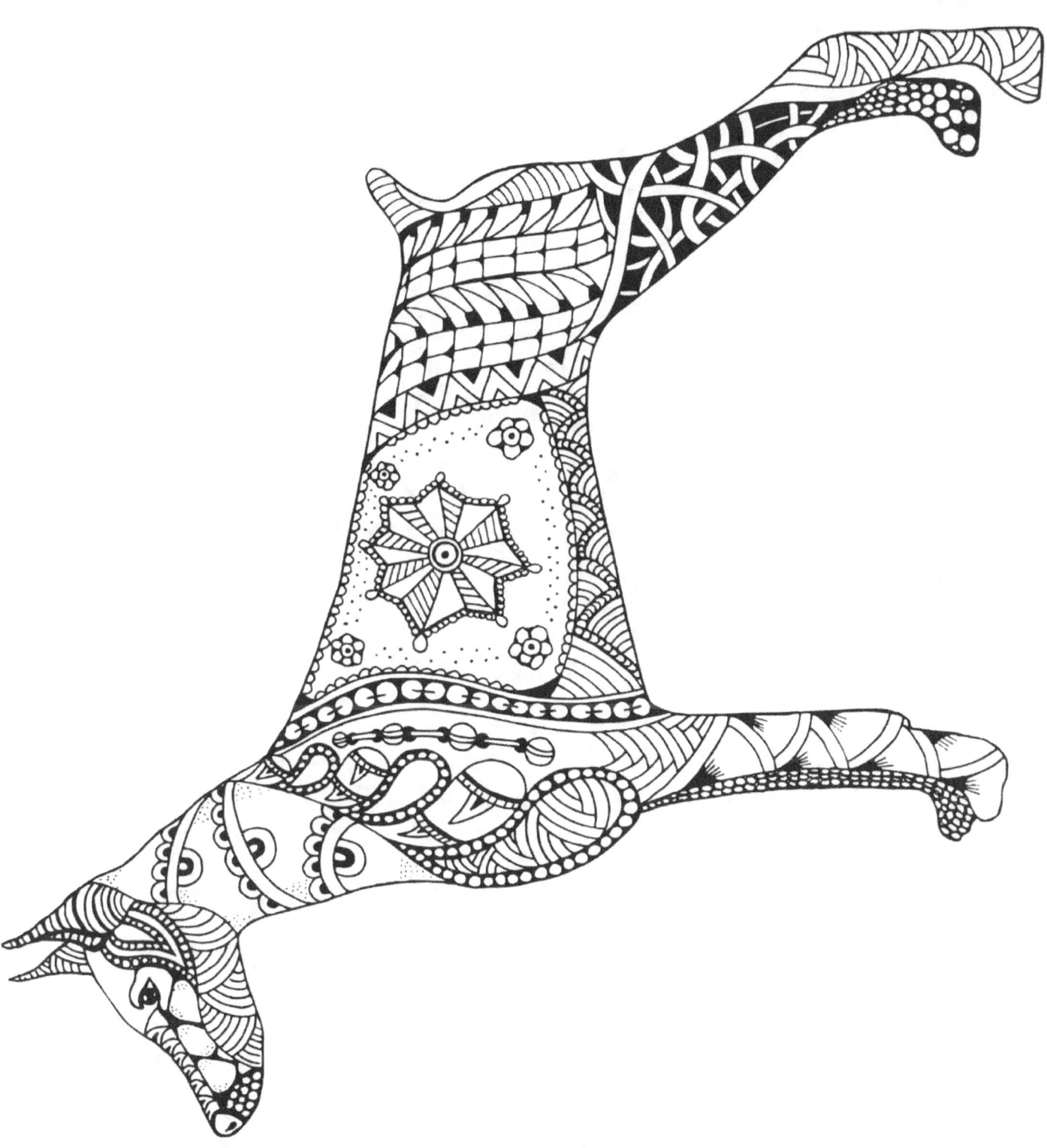

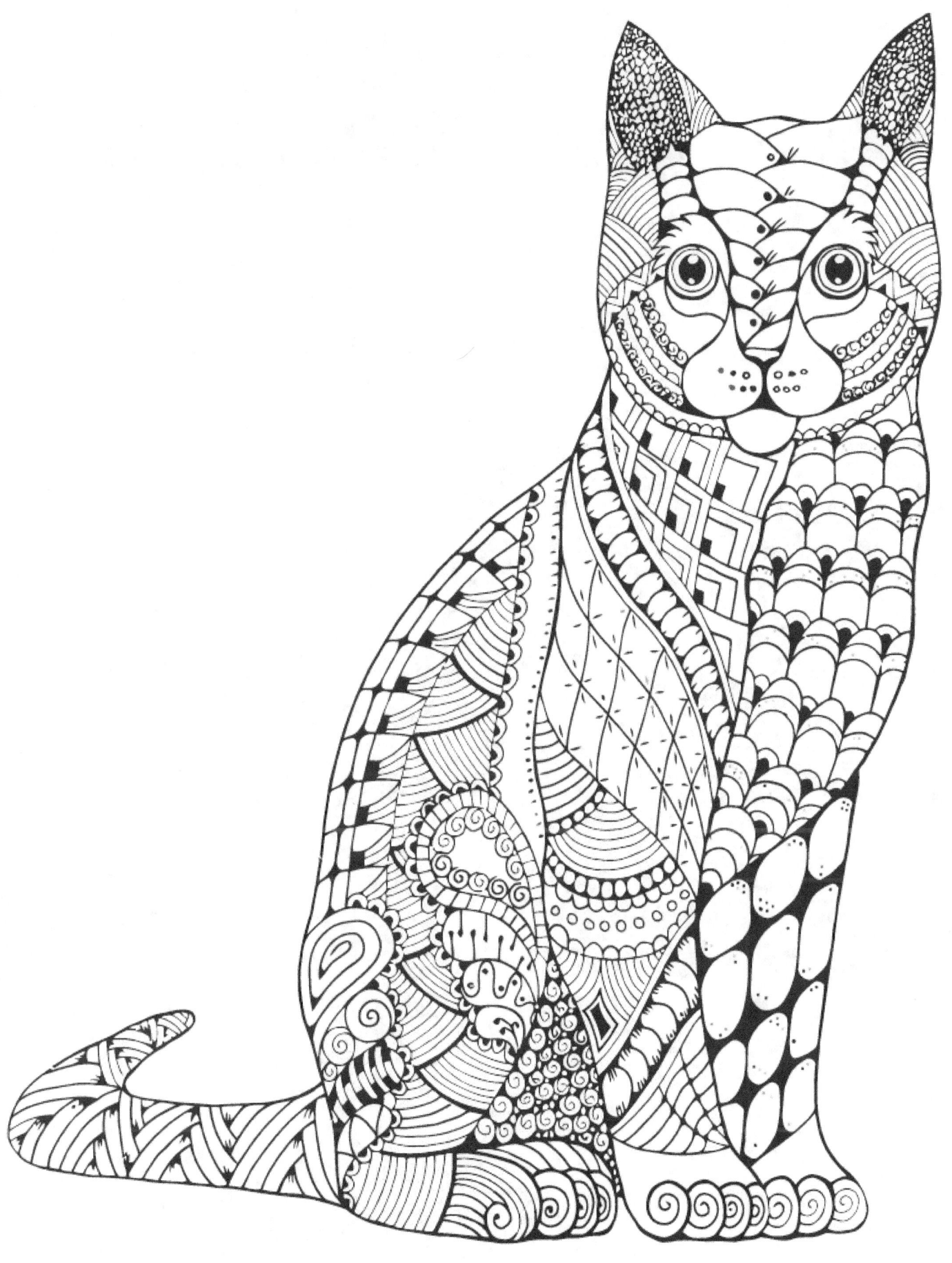

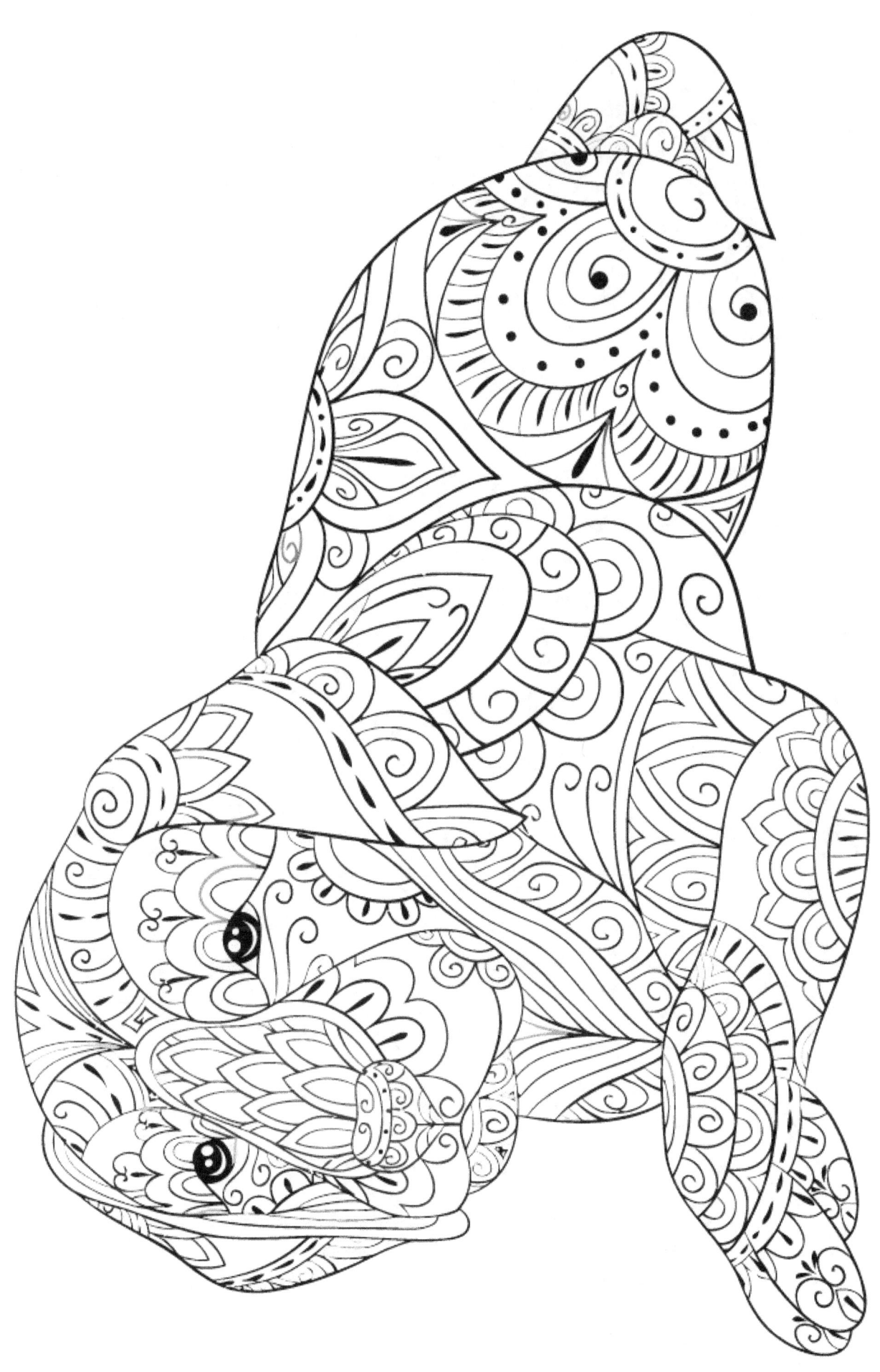

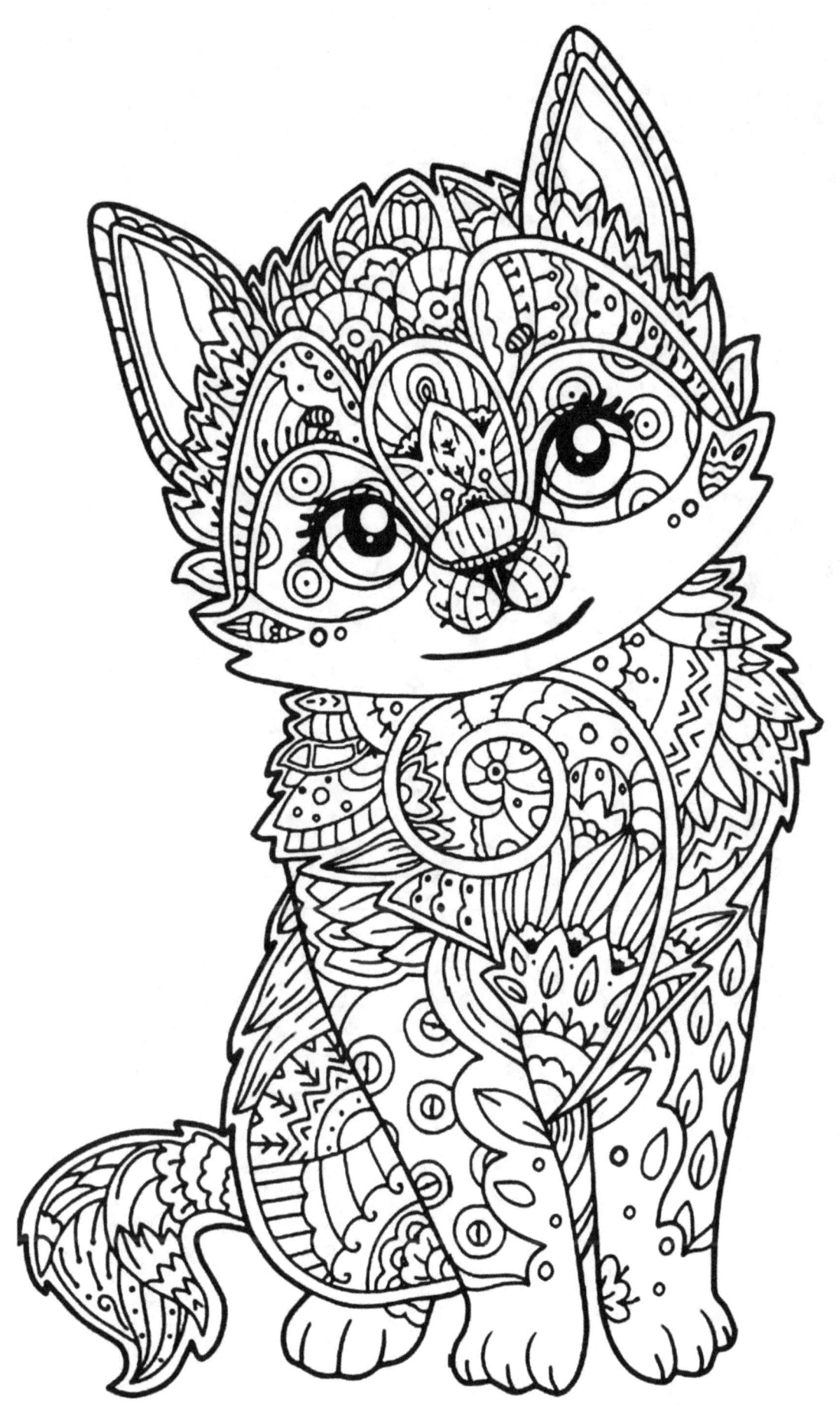

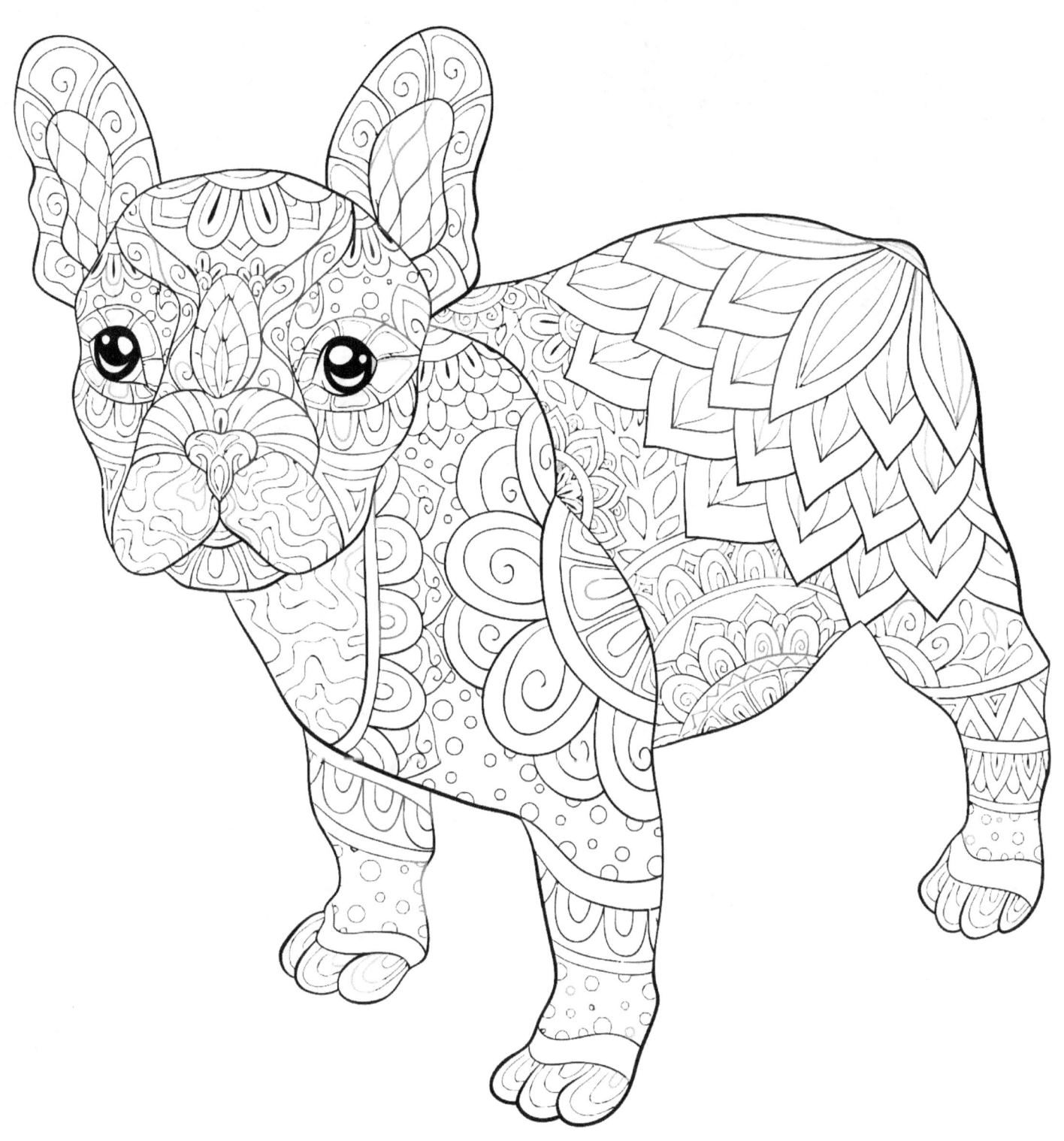

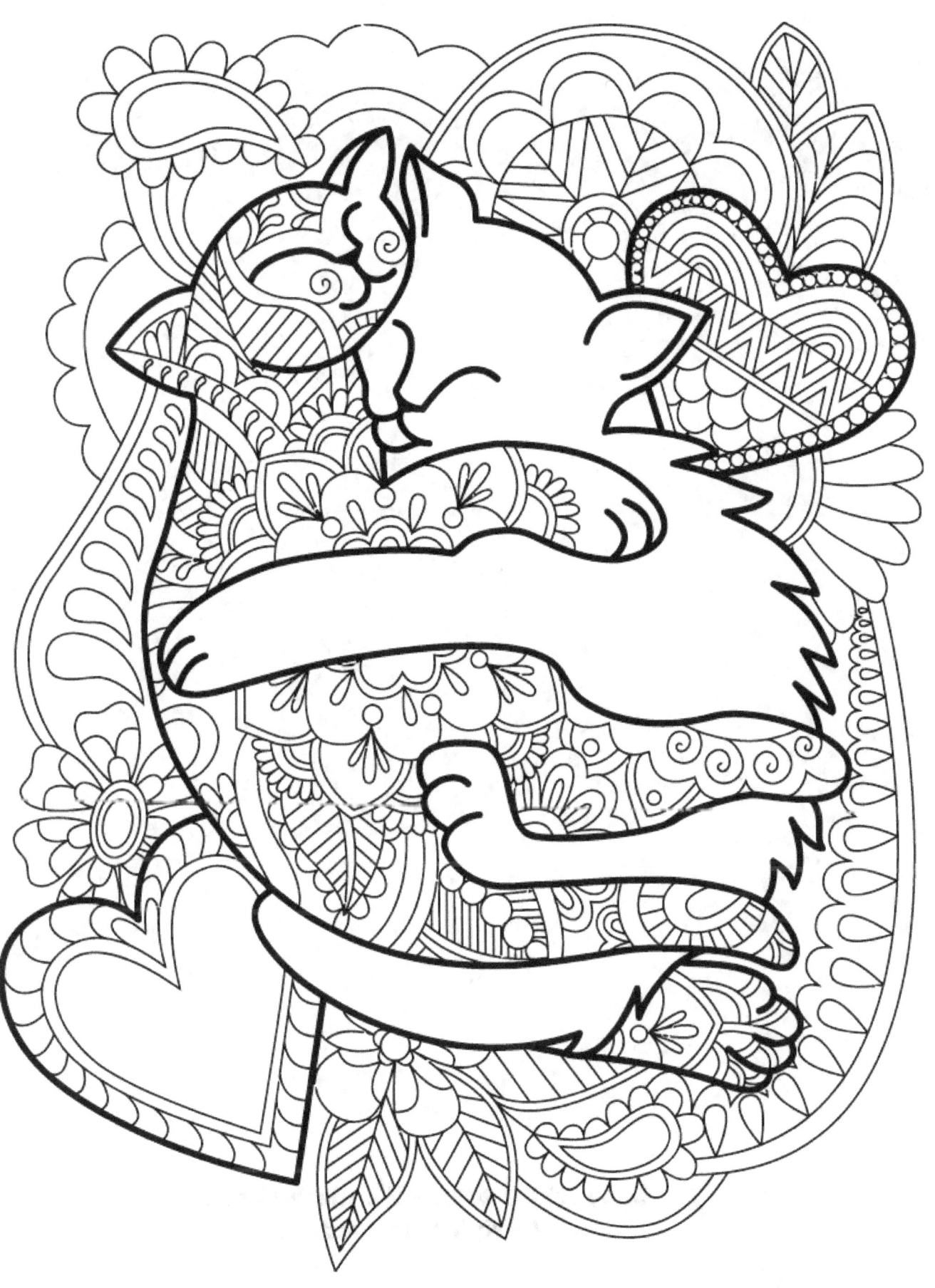

Copyright © 2022 – Wonderful Press
All rights reserved.

www.ingramcontent.com/pod-product-compliance
Lightning Source LLC
Chambersburg PA
CBHW080507220526
45465CB00006B/2403